Fresh Faced Beauty

Alex Brennan

Fresh
Faced
Beauty

MAKE YOUR OWN BATH,
BODY & HAIRCARE RECIPES
FOR A HEALTHY GLOW

PAVILION

Recipe Menu

HANDS 28
All-Natural Soap (Lye-Free) 30
Nourishing Hand Sanitizer 32
Walnut Whip Hand Soap 33
Lemon & Lime Hand Wash 34
Forever Young Lavender Hand Lotion 36
Honey & Vanilla Hand Lotion 37

SHAMPOO 38
Grapefruit & Coconut Milk Shampoo 42
Hair Rescue Cypress & Rosemary Shampoo 44
Revitalizing Citrus Shampoo 45
Cinnamon & Ginger Shampoo Bar 47
Volumizing Dry Shampoo 48

HAIR RINSES 50
Aromatic Vinegar Hair Rinse 52
Lavender Tea & Citrus Hair Rinse 53

HAIR CONDITIONERS 54
Coconut & Almond Conditioning Balm 56
Sweet Basil & Orange Conditioner 57

HAIR MASKS 58

HAIR STYLING 62
Citrus Hair Gel 64
Botanical Texturizing Spray 65
Orange & Cardamom Hair Spray 66

THE BODY BEAUTIFUL 68
Hydrating Bath Milk 70
Muscle Relief Bath Salts 72
Calming Bedtime Bubble Bath 73
Lavender & Rose Body Conditioner 74
Feel Good Bath Tablets 76
Sensual Body Wash 78
Jojoba & Peppermint Foot Scrub 79
Orange & Pomegranate Body Scrub 81
Coco Blast Body Scrub 83
Spiced Coffee Rejuvenating Body Oil 84
Revitalizing Body Butter 86
Gentle Vegan Body Butter 87
Healing Body Butter 88
Sunburnt Skin Rescue 89
The 'Anti' Antiperspirant 90

LIPS & MOUTH 92
Spearmint Lip Scrub 94
Tropical Lip Balm 95
Peppermint Toothpaste 96
Minty Antibacterial Mouth Wash 98

CELLULITE BE GONE 100
Coconut Coffee Scrub Cakes for Cellulite 106

SO LONG STRETCH MARKS 108

STAYING FUZZ-FREE 112
My Favourite Homemade Shaving Cream 116
Easy DIY Shaving Cream 118
Bikini Beautiful Skin Mask 120

A Love Letter

Let me tell you a story... Four years ago, amidst a series of hugely stressful events and when I was trying to make a name for myself in the modelling world, all my hair started falling out. Stress can do unexpected things to the body, and it's not uncommon for cells to go on strike. But a model with no hair isn't something you see every day. After a dozen doctor's visits and specialist appointments, I was disheartened and depressed; everyone could tell me what was wrong (alopecia), but not how to fix it. When all hope seemed lost, a dear friend suggested I look at the ingredients in my shampoo. Isopropyl alcohol, propylene glycol, sodium lauryl sulphate... holy moly! I mean, this was hazmat-suit stuff. What the hell were these ingredients and had I really put them on my scalp day after day?

In the end I took matters into my own hands and, armed with bottles of homemade shampoo and conditioner, my hair finally grew back. Then I started to really look at the state of the rest of my body – problematic skin, allergies, cellulite. Simple, one-ingredient, healthy alternatives – bought in supermarkets and health-food stores – have changed not just the quality of my skin but also my overall health.

Fast forward to today and I'm still outraged that nothing has changed in the beauty industry. Sure, we've got the organic movement flooding the airwaves but have you had a look at the ingredients in those products? Many of them are as aggressive as their non-organic counterparts, not to mention being murder on your wallet! My products offer sweet relief and now even friends who are make-up artists and models use them at home and on the job.

Learning and practising natural skin care has been amazingly beneficial and super EASY! If I can do it; you can do it. It's as simple as that! That first bottle of homemade shampoo changed my life and now I want to share with you all the little tips, tricks that I've discovered along the way. This book is for anyone and everyone who wants to make a change, and I'm so honoured to teach you everything I know.

Lots of love,

Alex Brennan

Introduction

We spend a lot of our waking life (even part of our sleeping, if you count loo breaks in the night) in the bathroom. It's often the most used room in the house and it's one of my favourites; in fact, I choose my home based on the bathroom and kitchen. If, like me, you couldn't do without a bath tub, I hope you'll love my recipes for bath-time treats as much as I do.

The products you keep in your porcelain room are as individual as your likes and dislikes in life. This book is dedicated to all those special little concoctions that no bathroom is complete without; some are 'essentials' and others are just for fun. Most of these DIYs are quick to make but if you want something that takes a second, just follow my #everyonelovesaquickie advice.

If you do a lot of travelling, then you'll know there's nothing better than your own shower (and your own bed), and while I'm usually fine with sleeping in foreign places, I never can get used to the unfamiliarity of a hotel bathroom. Perhaps it's because we tend to enter dirty and leave clean, but nothing reminds you you're away from home quite like the idea that someone else (someone you don't know, no less) has used that pristine sanctuary. Whenever I find myself somewhere new, the first thing I do is unpack all my little beauty products and place them around the bathroom, then I run the shower (or the bath if they have one) and add a few drops of my favourite essential oil (ylang ylang) to the water. Instantly I feel more at home.

If you're on the road and don't want to take a mountain of products with you, then I recommend packing a shampoo bar (see page 47). You can use it for your whole body (hair to feet) and it weighs so little you'll have more space for shopping.

Personal hygiene covers more than just washing your hands or brushing your teeth: it's a whole-body affair. To make life easy I've split this book into body-specific sections, so whatever products you'd find in your bathroom now, I've got you covered.

'Learn with your mind, listen with your body'

Four years ago, when my awakening began, a dear friend taught me the value of listening as well as learning. Anyone who's ever been on a diet knows that you have to learn to ignore your own desires – your body is hungry but you pretend you can't hear it; it's not your tummy grumbling, it must be an echo. Learning to ignore my own thoughts, feelings and impulses was how I ended up in all this mess.

If you'd asked me back then what was 'wrong' with me, I could've rattled off a list of carefully studied diagnoses I'd been given; I could even have told you all the ways to 'cure' them; but if you'd asked me how I was feeling there'd have been silence. I wasn't oblivious to my emotions, I just plain didn't want to acknowledge them – sometimes pain does funny things to people.

Part of removing all the questionable chemicals in my house and testing a bunch of recipes was learning how to listen. How could I know my body was not ok if I never gave it a chance to tell me?

In this magical era, where we hustle and bustle day in, day out and human contact comes in the form of texts, emails and Instagram feeds, I think we are all a little guilty of neglecting ourselves. Ever thought to yourself, 'I just don't have the time'? There's a reason ready-made everything is available, whether it's pre-packaged, drive-through, home delivery or ordered online; trust me, I get it, but it's also the reason suppliers never have to change their products. Humans are busy, ergo they'll keep buying what they don't have to make. Let's get this straight, I'm not one of those knit-your-own-breakfast types with too much time on my hands – I'm drawn to convenience as much as anybody else. When I started creating products, I made a shampoo and a conditioner and that was it. For six months I carried on using all the other regular rubbish I'd been buying for as long as I can remember, but the ongoing task of listening to my body meant I eventually had no choice but to throw them away and go back to basics. I could feel something wasn't right and even though my hair had begun to grow back (in great condition, I might add), my skin was a mess, I had cellulite, I was tired all the time and I was developing allergies left, right and centre.

I pulled all the beauty products out of my cupboards and laid them on the floor of my lounge room (a little excessive perhaps but hey, that's me). I had a notepad and pen next to me and carefully wrote down every ingredient I didn't know, had never heard of, or just plain sounded dodgy. It took hours!

When I'd finally compiled my list I sat down at the computer – ok in truth I took a nap, watched a couple of DVDs and chilled out – but when all of that was done, I set to work and between me and Google I had a fair description of each ingredient. On my last ingredient – DBP, I stumbled upon a website called the Skin Deep Database (www.ewg. org/skindeep), a comprehensive list of every chemical (organic and traditional) ever used in cosmetics, skin care and perfumes. Talk about hitting the jackpot – this was everything I was looking for and more…

The Terrible 'Touch-me-nots'

Also known as the 'dirty dozen', this is a glossary of AVOIDS in beauty products. (Quick warning – this is going to read a little like a science lecture as these ingredients are specialized chemicals.)

Every day we use products that we think are ok; but in truth most are not proven to be safe, and manufacturers don't have to tell us so. Neither the EU or the FDA (Food and Drug Administration) require pre-market approval of beauty and cosmetic products and ingredients, so products could be marketed without government approval, regardless of what tests show. There are 25,000 chemicals used in cosmetics and most have not been tested for long-term effects.

Who knew?! I know I didn't until my own health was affected. It's best to always read the labels and know what's in your products. Don't be scared… just get educated and avoid the baddies on the list below.

BHA AND BHT
Used as preservatives, there are concerns that these are toxic to organs and cause irritation to the skin, eyes and lungs. BHA has been linked to endocrine disruption.

COAL TAR DERIVATIVES
Many synthetic colours are derived from coal tar and are potentially carcinogenic. Look out for p-phenylenediamine – used in numerous hair dyes - and colours with the prefix D&C or FD&C.

DEA, MEA AND TEA
Keep an eye out for any ingredients that include the acronyms DEA, MEA and TEA (diethanolamine, monoethanolamine and triethanolamine respectively). These are used as surfactants and they carry several health concerns, the most worrying of which is that they can increase the risk for cancer.

DIBUTYL PHTHALATE (DBP)
Used as a plasticizer, fragrance ingredient and solvent, this acts as an endocrine disrupter and can cause damage to the reproductive system. The EU has banned its use in cosmetics.

FORMALDEHYDE
This carcinogen can be released by several different preservatives used in the cosmetics industry, namely DMDM hydantoin, diazolidinyl urea, imidazolidinyl urea, methenamine, quaternium-15 and sodium hydroxymethylglycinate. Low-level use of these ingredients is permitted but in the EU a product containing over 0.05 per cent formaldehyde must carry the warning 'contains formaldehyde' on the label.

PARABENS
This family of preservatives has gained a lot of negative publicity in recent years and rightly so; they mimic oestrogen and can disrupt the endocrine system that regulates our hormones.

PARFUM/FRAGRANCE
These terms when used on cosmetics ingredients labels are unbelievably vague: they can refer to any mixture of synthetic fragrances which don't have to be named individually. They are associated with allergic reactions, asthma and respiratory problems.

PEGS
A.k.a. polyethylene glycols, these are derived from petroleum and are used in many skin cream bases. Impurities such as 1,4-dioxane, found in may PEG compounds, have been linked to cancer.

PETROLATUM
Obtained from petroleum and used in some hair products for shine and as a moisture barrier in some lip balms, lipsticks and moisturizers. Associated with organ system toxicity; also has contamination concerns.

SILOXANES
Any ingredient ending in '-siloxane' or '-methicone'. Used in a variety of cosmetics to soften and moisten. There are various concerns around endocrine disruption and organ toxicity.

SODIUM LAURETH/LAURYL SULPHATE (SLES/SLS)
These foaming agents have been known to cause irritation to the skin, eyes and lungs. They may be contaminated with ethylene oxide and 1,4-dioxane, which may increase the risk for cancer.

TRICLOSAN
A preservative and anti-bacterial agent that is found in toothpastes, cleansers and antiperspirants. Irritating to the skin and eyes and suspected of hormone disruption.

The Ins & Outs of the Organic Movement

'I couldn't find anything on the market free of harmful ingredients so I decided to create my own.'
Heard this before? It is, of course, the line used by every 'organic' skin-care brand that comes along.
The organic movement isn't all bad – it's definitely a step in the right direction – but what if I told you that just because an ingredient comes from the Earth it doesn't make it healthy? Shocked? So was I! Now, I'm a huge fan of Mother Nature and what she offers, but not everything growing is meant for us. This is why I get a little red-faced when talking about organic product companies as I tend to find they use ingredients that no one really looks into, and then slap a massive price tag on. Let me show you what I mean. Meet the top four 'organic' beauty ingredients...

Cetearyl Alcohol

What it's used for Emulsifier, emollient, foam booster, stabilizer, thickener.

Avoid it because Possible eye, lung and skin irritant.

What it's made from Originally derived from sperm-whale oil, but now comes from palm oil.

Alex weighs in A long time ago I ordered a bucket of cetearyl alcohol to experiment with. When it was heated it smelled absolutely horrendous. The warning labels were a bit off-putting, too: 'Do not get in contact with skin', 'Do not get in contact with eyes', 'Do not breathe dust.' So.. a product that's usually in lotions shouldn't be in contact with skin? Yes, it gets diluted, but wouldn't you rather use a moisturizer that has ingredients you don't have to worry about?

Propylene Glycol

What it's used for Thickener, filler.

Avoid it because It has just about every side effect: the risk of cancer, reproductive toxicity, usage restrictions, allergies and immune system toxicity, skin and eye irritations, organ system toxicity, endocrine disruption and neurotoxicity. It is also a penetration enhancer, meaning it penetrates skin cells, getting right into the bloodstream, carrying other chemicals with it.

What it's made from Derived from glycerine.

Alex weighs in If you're using a supposedly 'natural' deodorant, odds are it contains propylene glycol. Many of the natural companies sell 'paraben-free' and 'aluminium-free' deodorants, but they still contain propelyne glycol because it's a cheap ingredient that makes a clear and thick deodorant bar.

Tocopheryl Acetate

What it's used for Antioxidant agent, labelling appeal (it is often listed as Vitamin E Acetate).

Avoid it because Certain studies suggest that it's toxic on skin and other organs. The biggest concern is that it can be contaminated in the manufacturing process by hydroquinone, a chemical that is highly toxic and carcinogenic in high concentrations.

What it's made from Made by combining natural vitamin E with acetic acid.

Alex weighs in 'Now with vitamin E!' sounds great on a label. This form of vitamin E has a longer shelf life and it's cheaper than natural vitamin E which is why companies use it. What they're not telling you is that it has risks for contamination and that it's a skin irritant and toxin. Some companies even try to pass this nasty chemical off as a 'natural' ingredient.

Limonene and Linalool

These little fellows are in every organic product under the sun. Limonene is a colourless liquid hydrocarbon derived from citrus peels and linalool is an alcohol found in flowers and spice plants. Sound ok? Well...

Limonene is believed to disrupt the body's ability to regulate serotonin and dopamine (the happy hormones), and so may be linked to depression and anxiety. Linalool breaks down when mixed with oxygen, forming a toxic by-product that can cause skin disorders, stress and brain malfunction.

The Harmful, the Organic & the Natural Alternatives

Below is a list of every necessary ingredient in cosmetics and skin care; the harmful, the organic (yep, still harmful) and the all-natural substitute. Next time you're swayed to buy the organic product or if you already have a shelf-full take a closer look and see how many contain these naughties.

Unfortunately, the word 'natural' has little meaning when it comes to cosmetics labelling, which is why it's important to know what all the ingredients on the label are so you can make an informed decision about what you're putting on your skin. Remember, ingredients are listed from highest percentage to lowest.

COLOURS OR COLOURANTS

Coal-tar derived colours in cosmetics are a concern because coal tar is a carcinogen. Some colour additives are not approved for food products, but may be added to cosmetics such as lipstick, which are inevitably ingested.

Look out for (and avoid):
Aluminum lakes, astaxanthin, azulene, canthaxanthin, sodium copper chlorophyllin (chlorophyll), D&C / FD&C colours, p-phenylenediamine, ultramarine.

Natural alternatives?
The above are used in many so-called 'natural' and 'organic' products so always read the ingredients list. True natural alternatives include beet powder, annatto, henna and caramel. Mica powders and iron oxides also have natural components and are non-toxic and non-irritating.

EMOLLIENTS

Emollients prevent moisture loss. Some synthetic emollients do not allow the skin to breathe and can actually cause it to become irritated and dehydrated.

Look out for (and avoid):
Acetylated lanolin alcohol, butyl adipate, capric/caprylic triglyceride, ceteareth, cetearyl alcohol, cetyl esters, cetyl palmitate, coconut fatty acids, cyclomethicone, decyl oleate, dicaprylate-dicapriate, dimethicone, disodium, cocoamphodiacetate, dodecatrienol, eucerin (petroleum jelly), glycerol-mono-stearate-palmitate, glyceryl cocoate, glyceryl stearate, hydrated palm glycerides, hydrogenated oils, isobutyl stearate, isopropyl lanolate, isopropyl myristate, isostearyl-isostearate, lauryl lactate, octyl palmitate, octyldodecanol, oleth-2, paraffin, petrolatum, squalane, stearate, stearyl alcohol.

Natural alternatives?
Plant oils such as almond oil, avocado oil, coconut oil, hazelnut oil, jojoba oil, olive oil, safflower oil, sesame oil, sunflower oil and tamanu oil. Shea butter, cocoa butter and beeswax are also natural emollients.

HUMECTANTS

Many synthetic humectants (to soften skin) draw moisture from the lower layers of skin but fail to replace it, giving softer skin in the short term, but drying it out over time.

Look out for (and avoid):
Butylene glycol, ethylene / diethylene glycol, PEG compounds (e.g. polyethylene glycol), polypropylene glycol, propylene glycol.

Natural alternatives?
Natural humectants deliver moisture to the lower levels of skin while also attracting moisture to the surface. Aloe, lecithin and vegetable glycerine are among them.

EMULSIFIERS

Emulsifiers either suspend tiny drops of oil in water (used in creams and lotions) or water within oil (used in heavier creams). They are often derived from petrochemical gases and as such can irritate the skin.

Look out for (and avoid):
Acetylated lanolin alcohol, alkyl polyglycoside, cetearyl alcohol, betaine, carbomer, carboxymethyl cellulose, cocamidopropyl betaine (coco betaine), ethyl acetate, ethylene glycol distearate, fatty acid alkanolamide, glyceryl mono-di-oleate, glycerol mono-di-stearate, PEG-100 stearate, PEG-25 hydrogenated castor oil, polysorbate, sodium lauryl sulphate, sodium sulfosuccinates, sorbitan esters, sorbitan stearate, stearyl alcohol, triethanolamine (TEA).

Natural alternatives?
Lecithin, jojoba oil, carnauba wax and rice bran.

FRAGRANCES

Synthetic fragrances are mainly derived from petroleum sources. The word 'fragrance' or 'parfum' on a label can refer to any mixture of synthetic fragrances which may cause allergies, dermatitis and breathing problems.

Look out for (and avoid):
Amyl acetate (banana fragrance), anisole, benzophenones 1 to 12 (rose fragrance), berry fragrance, bitter almond oil (benzaldehyde), cinnamic acid, coconut fragrance, cucumber fragrance, honeysuckle fragrance, lilac fragrance (anisyl acetate), mango fragrance, melon fragrance, methyl acetate (apple fragrance), methyl salicylate (wintergreen or birch fragrance), plum fragrance, peach fragrance, phenethyl alcohol / phenoxyethanol (rose fragrance), strawberry fragrance, vanillin, verataldehyde (vanilla fragrance).

Natural alternatives?
Don't be fooled by 'natural fragrance' – the only way to avoid synthetic fragrances is to stick with certified organic essential oils. Happily, there are masses to choose from.

PRESERVATIVES

Even though nature provides its own preservatives, cosmetics companies favour cheaply produced synthetic equivalents, including parabens, which disrupt hormone levels; and diazolidinyl/imidazoidinyl urea and DMDM hydantoin, which release formaldehyde, a toxic chemical.

Look out for (and avoid):
Ascorbic acid, ascorbyl palmitate, benzethonium chloride, benzyl alcohol, BHA, BHT, boric acid, butyl paraben, captan, cetrimonium bromide, chloramine, chlorhexidine, chlorobutanol, chloroxylenol, chlorphenesin, diazolidinyl urea, DMDM hydantoin, ethanolamines, ethyl paraben, euxyl, germaben, germall, hexachlorophene, imidazolidinyl urea, isopropyl alcohol, kathon, methenamine, methyl paraben, methylisothiazolinone, phenethyl alcohol, phenoxyethanol, phenylphenol, potassium metabisulfite, propyl paraben, quaternary ammonium compounds, salicylic acid, SD alcohol, sodium bisulfite, sodium borate,

sodium hydroxymethylglycinate, sodium propionate, sorbic acid, succinic acid, thimerosal, undecylenic acid.

Natural alternatives?
Tea tree essential oil, thyme essential oil, grapefruit seed extract, bitter orange extract, honey.

SOLVENTS

Water is the most natural solvent (used to dissolve ingredients and extract fragrance) in the world. But not all ingredients dissolve in water, so cosmetics' companies may use synthetic solvents instead. These can leave a chemical residue that can irritate the skin, eyes and lungs.

Look out for (and avoid):
Acetic acid, acetone, amyl alcohol, benzene, butylene glycol, ethyl alcohol (synthetic), ethyl butyl acetate, ethylene glycol monophenyl-ether (phenoxyethanol), glycerine, hexane, isopropyl alcohol, methanol, phenol, propyl alcohol, propylene glycol, SD alcohols.

Natural alternatives?
Water, apple cider vinegar, grain alcohol.

SURFACTANTS

Surfactants (surface-acting agents) thicken and create foam in shampoos and skin cleansers. Sodium lauryl sulphate is the poster (bad) boy here and along with DEA, TEA or MEA compounds can irritate the skin and scalp.

Look out for (and avoid):
Ammonium lauryl sulphate, betaine, carboxylate, cocamide DEA or MEA, cocamidopropyl betaine, cocamidopropyl hydroxysultaine, cocamine, cocoamphoglycinate, cococarboxamide

MEA-4-carboxylate, coconut and corn oil 'soap', coconut betaine, coconut surfactants (ammonium lauryl or laureth sulphate), coco polyglucose, DEA cetyl phosphate, decyl glucoside, decyl oleate, decyl polyglucose, diethanolamine (DEA), disodium lauryl sulfosuccinate, glyceryl cocoate, glycerol laurate, glycerol monolaurate, glycerol stearate, lactamide DEA, lauramide DEA/MEA, magnesium lauryl sulphate, methyl glucose dioleate, neutralized coconut extract, olefin sulfonate, PEG-100 (polyethylene glycol) stearate, PEG-150 (polyethylene glycol) distearate, sodium coco sulphate, sodium cocoyl isethionate, sodium laureth sulphate, sodium lauryl sulphate, sodium myreth sulphate, sodium myristoyl sarcosinate, sodium stearate, sorbitan stearate, sucrose cocoate, sulphated/sulfonated oil, TEA (triethanolamine) lauryl sulphate, sodium cocoamphodiacetate, sodium cocoyl glutamate, sodium lauryl sarcosinate.

Natural alternatives?
Castile soap (made only from vegetable oils), and natural foaming agents including yucca extract, soapwort and quillaja bark extract.

THICKENERS

We've been brainwashed to think that thicker creams, shampoos and conditioners are more luxurious, but in fact some thickeners carry contamination concerns.

Look out for (and avoid):
Carbomer, cocamide DEA or MEA, hydrolyzed wheat protein, hydroxymethyl cellulose, hydroxypropyl cellulose, methacryloyl ethyl betaine, methacrylates copolymer, oat protein, potassium stearate, quinoa protein, soy protein, vegetable cellulose.

Natural alternatives?
Locust bean gum, guar gum, acacia gum, clay minerals.

Before You Begin, a Detox Like No Other

We all know about detoxifying the body of diet nasties, but what about removing harmful chemicals that we absorb through the skin? Here's my body detox: put all your bathtime, cleansing and skincare products away and stick to the four essentials below – for a weekend at least – then start experimenting with other natural alternatives. At the start, you may notice an increased sensitivity to the scent of mass-market products: it didn't take long for me to find the smell of my once-favourite shampoo sickly sweet and the whiff of synthetic perfumes really overpowering. After detoxing, though, I felt healthier and my skin and hair were thankful that they were no longer doused in unnecessary chemicals.

The following four products are all you'll need at the start:

1. PURE CASTILE SOAP
As a body wash, shampoo and hand soap, all in one.

2. BICARBONATE OF SODA (BAKING SODA)
As a face wash and toothpaste.

3. COCONUT OIL
As a moisturizer and lotion.

4. SALT AND SUGAR
If you need to exfoliate.

TOP TIPS FOR YOUR DETOX

Detoxifying your beauty routine is less intimidating than it seems. Here are my top tips to ease the way.

PREPARE YOURSELF (ROUND 1)
Your body is removing a bunch of ickies. Relax! Oiliness, fatigue, low mood and headaches are all normal reactions. Curl up with a book until your body re-balances.

DRINK UP
Your body is more than 70-per-cent water. We store toxins and water in our cells – keeping your fluids replenished will help eliminate some of the nasties.

TAKE A CLAY SHOT
Bentonite clay is a positively charged element so it attaches like a magnet to negative elements – like all those iddy-biddy chemicals your body's been absorbing. A teaspoon of clay mixed with ½ cup water twice a day will get those nasties out quick-smart (see note, page 26).

BATHE AWAY
Epsom salts draw out excess fluid, the very place we hold toxins. A 20-minute soak in a tub with ½ cup of Epsom salts will do wonders for removing any chemical build-up.

BE IN IT FOR THE LONG HAUL
There's not much point detoxing just to retox again later. Post detox, start integrating all-natural products into your routine (it's ok if it takes a little time – baby steps).

LISTEN REAL GOOD
These days I meditate twice a day to check in with how I'm feeling. Try adding a little practice before bed and listen to your body's messages about what you need.

PREPARE YOURSELF (ROUND 2)
Your body will take a little time to chill on its production of the natural lubricants it's been making to compensate for the chemicals that have been stripping it bare. Give your body two weeks to calm itself – you'll probably be a little shiny and oily for a while. Be patient! I promise it's worth it.

READY TO RUN?

I remember the first time I told someone I made my own beauty products, he replied, 'For some reason, I've just got images of you making soap from rendered fat like in Fight Club'. If you've seen the film (heck, even if you haven't) it doesn't really sound like the type of thing you want to be doing or maybe even something you're capable of.

I'm not a chemist, or a dermatologist, or any manner of '-ist', I'm just an ordinary girl who uses her kitchen to make food that's wearable as opposed to edible (to be fair, you can actually eat most of these, but they taste pretty awful). These recipes are generally really easy, and I mean 'a five-year-old could do it' kind of easy, and you can buy many of the ingredients at your local supermarket.

If you want to keep it simple or you're concerned all this is over your head, start your journey with the #everyonelovesaquickie recipes – they're mostly one (supermarket) ingredient, which you can add to your weekly shop. The rest of the recipes are graded into three levels (see opposite) so you can start wherever you feel most comfortable. The point really is to have fun and when you've found your rhythm, go ahead and kick some 'advanced' recipe's butt!

Easy as One, Two, Three

The recipes are labelled 'easy', 'medium' or 'advanced', so you can see at a glance the amount of time and effort involved. Happily, most of the recipes are a piece of cake – much less work than baking a cake, in fact! Always read through the recipe before you start and be sure you have all the necessary ingredients and equipment to hand.

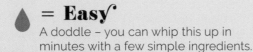

= Easy
A doddle – you can whip this up in minutes with a few simple ingredients.

= Medium
A little more time and effort required – and maybe the odd specialized ingredient.

= Advanced
Something of a labour of love – but the results are totally worth it!

Every Beauty Cook's Arsenal

If you're going to cook, you're going to need ingredients. These beauty heroes are your staples; you can use them alone, as well as in multiple recipes in this book, and they're easy to find.

Coconut Oil

This wonder ingredient is naturally antibacterial and antifungal, and what's more, it's a brilliant moisturizer, so it's no surprise that it's used as the base of all sorts of natural beauty products. Coconut oil is a healthy oil for cooking with, too, and most supermarkets now stock it. I recommend keeping two jars – one in the kitchen and one in the bathroom!

Cocoa Butter

This creamy coloured fat is extracted from the cocoa bean in the process of making chocolate. It's edible, melts at body temperature and its moisturizing powers make it a great addition to natural beauty recipes. There's a surprising number of supermarkets that carry cocoa butter as it's quite delicious in cakes and homemade chocolate, but if you can't find it, try a health-food store or online.

Arrowroot Powder

A white starchy powder, made from the rhizomes of the arrowroot plant, *Maranta arundinacea*. Handy to have in the kitchen cupboard for gluten-free baking, it's also a key ingredient in natural deodorant and dry shampoo. The cheapest and easiest way to source arrowroot powder is from your local supermarket (if you can't find it, you can use cornflour instead).

Essential Oils

These naturally derived aromatic oils last for years and can be used individually or in a blend to infuse DIY beauty recipes with beautiful fragrance. I purchase them online because it's easier to find all the aromas I want without ever leaving my house. Use those that are certified organic.

Beeswax

A wondrous natural, non-toxic ingredient that has incredibly useful properties for skincare, beeswax helps to thicken creams and works as a protectant and humectant, providing great staying power. I use beeswax in lotions, lotion bars, lip balm and foot cream. The good stuff has a mild honey scent. Some supermarkets stock this as it's great for polishing wood, but if not, try a health-food store or online.

Liquid Castile Soap

Aside from being a base for heaps of recipes, liquid Castile soap (made from vegetable oils) can actually be used alone for everything. You can clean the house with it, use it as a body wash, shampoo, for making baby wipes and much more. Find it online or in health-food stores. I use Dr Bronner's.

Liquid Carrier Oil

Sometimes you need a thinner base than coconut oil or cocoa butter, and that's where liquid carrier oils come in. I use them for smoother lotions, baby oil, salves and after-shave balms. My favourites are sweet almond oil and jojoba oil, but you can actually use store-bought extra virgin olive oil.

Shea Butter

This has amazing healing properties and can be used to cure skin rashes and acne; reduce scars, stretch marks, and peeling after tanning; soothe frost bite and burns; and reduce arthritic pain and muscle fatigue. You can find shea butter in health-food stores or online – just make sure it's unscented and unrefined.

Equipment

You don't need any fancy equipment to make the recipes in this book, in fact you probably already have most of these items in your kitchen. If not, you can find them in cookware stores or online and yes, it's completely fine to use the same equipment for food and beauty – after all the ingredients are healthy enough to eat!

Hand Mixer Also known as a stick blender, this is useful for a bunch of things but I find with product making it's more effective (and less tiring) than using a hand whisk.

Coffee Grinder My current grinder is so old I'm not actually sure where it's from. It's best to have a grinder just for your beauty ingredients, to avoid all your products smelling of coffee! For the recipes in this book, you may just about get away with a pestle and mortar, but if you're thinking larger quantities – a grinder is definitely best.

Water Filter This is really a judgement call. It's not essential, but I prefer to either filter or to once-boil and cool my tap water to remove chlorine and fluoride, which can wreak havoc with your skin, before using the water in my homemade products. If you don't have a filter (or just can't be bothered) using straight tap water is fine.

Measuring Spoons You can pick these up quite easily at any homeware store and my favourites are the set of five sizes all joined together. I recommend using wood or plastic as opposed to metal so there's no need for double sets when it comes to bentonite clay – which can't touch metal EVER! (See safety note, page 26.)

Double Boiler The best way to heat ingredients gently. You simmer water in the lower pan and place the ingredient you want to melt in the upper one. If you don't have a dedicated double boiler, simply place a heatproof bowl over a saucepan and you're good to go. You can allow the water to lap at the bowl, but don't let it flow over the edges of the pan.

Kitchen Scale These are the easiest way to be accurate in your measuring – and digital is best, especially when working with small quantities. Weights don't always have to be exact, but when making some lotions the difference of a gram can change the entire outcome of the recipe.

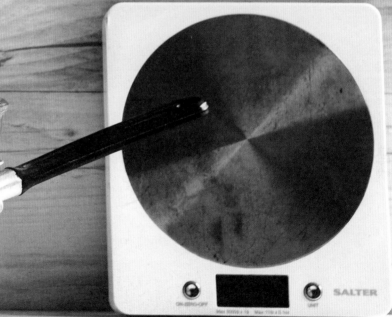

Jars & Bottles & Gifts... Oh My!

It's not necessary to buy specialist tubes or cosmetic containers for your products: any airtight bottles or jars from the pound or dollar store are perfectly fine – even old water bottles will work for your liquid creations. But if you'd like to package your products as gifts or make something that will take pride of place in your bathroom, here are some ideas.

Glass Jars

There's no better way to show off your handiwork than glass jars (plus they're environmentally friendly). Most pound or dollar stores have a variety of these in all shapes, sizes and colours at heavily discounted prices, otherwise homeware stores and some supermarkets stock them, too. When my product is on display it helps for the inside to look as pretty as the outside, so for body butters and yummy-looking recipes, I choose clear glass; otherwise opaque or coloured works well. Tie a ribbon around the top, add a handwritten label and you're all set.

Vases, Pots & Organizers

'Beauty in a pot' is one of the coolest concepts I've ever come across, and while I'd like to take credit for this original idea, it actually belongs to a friend's mum. All over her house she has decorated plant pots holding herbs, spices and powders; vases full of bath salts and bath milk; and organizer pots with chalk-style writing that seem to hold everything else. It's such a clever idea, and as the premise of these recipes is 'all natural', why not use something that signifies nature?

Tubes & Cosmetic Containers

Sometimes a jar is impractical and having my own product line, I know that some things really should be in proper containers. You can buy tubes for homemade hand lotions and soaps online and in some chemists and department stores (just ask for travel cosmetic containers). You can make your own sticky labels and the tubes will fit perfectly in little bags as a set.

Bottles

Reusable spray bottles, pump-top bottles and squeeze bottles are very handy. Glass bottles always look pretty and dark glass bottles are useful to protect essential oils from UV light. Dropper bottles are also brilliant for products that need to be dispensed in small quantities. I don't recommend using glass bottles for shower products such as shampoo, though, as the last thing you want is for them to fall and break.

KEEP IT STERILE

It's not a necessity, but if you want to be extra clean or help prolong shelf life, fill your container with 1 tsp rubbing alcohol (isopropyl alcohol) and fill the remainder with water. Give it a good shake, pour out the liquid and allow to dry.

DIY Kilner Jar Foaming Dispenser

I originally made this for the hand wash that sits in my bathroom and next to the kitchen sink, but now I use it for cleansers, shampoo and conditioner and even my body lotion. Kilner (Mason) jars are pretty cheap and you can now find them in several different pretty colours. I usually make my own little labels and cards for these so I remember what's in each one and when I'm using as a gift I customize them with photos and decorations individual to the giftee.

1-litre/32fl oz Kilner (Mason) jar with screw-top lid
Hammer and nail
Foaming soap dispenser pump (I used one from an old soap bottle)
Scissors
Couple of rubber bands

Using a permanent marker, make a mark in the centre of the jar lid. Place the tip of the nail on the mark and use the hammer to tap the nail and pierce a hole. NOTE: the nail can easily slip so please take care!

Use the hammer and nail to make more holes around the first hole, enlarging it until the dispenser pump sits snugly inside.

If the tube of the dispenser is too long for the jar, just trim it with a pair of scissors so it doesn't quite reach the bottom of the jar.

Wind a rubber band around the pump dispenser, directly under the lid. This is to form a seal to stop any soap escaping in case the jar tips over. You may need to add another rubber band to make a good seal.

Fill the jar with your product and screw on the lid.

#everyonelovesaquickie These days lots of stationery and discount stores sell glass 'drinking' jars with a hole pre-made for a straw. In the world of homemade beauty, these remove the need for hammer and nail, providing the perfect pre-perforated lid for a pump dispenser. Use an elastic band to create a seal around the pump stem if you need to.

Glossary

Alcohol Manufactured by fermenting sugars, widely used in perfumes, bathroom products and cosmetics and for making herbal medicines.

Allantoin A naturally occurring compound found in the comfrey plant. It helps heal wounds and skin ulcers.

Aloe Vera One of the most multi-tasking, health-promoting plants on Earth and can be both ingested and applied topically. It comes in juice, gel and powder forms.

Amino Acids There are 22 known amino acids, eight of which can't be produced by the body, and these are called essential amino acids. The body needs them in order to create its own proteins. In beauty products, amino acids are used to aid the metabolic processes in the skin and hair to repair and improve their condition.

Antioxidants Food compounds that neutralize chemicals called free radicals.

Apple Cider Vinegar The only alkaline vinegar, made by fermenting apple cider.

Arrowroot Powder A white, powdery starch that comes from tropical plants: the most common being *Maranta arundinacea*.

Bee Pollen This granular garnish is made by worker bees, who pack pollen into little granules with added honey or nectar.

Bicarbonate of Soda (Baking Soda) Bicarbonate of soda is a component of a natural mineral called natron which is found in mineral springs. It can be used for just about anything from deodorizing your shoes to easing indigestion.

Clays Fine-grained natural rock or soil material. Clay comes in different colours and varieties, including bentonite, kaolin and Australian beige clay.

Bentonite Clay
A WARNING!
Bentonite clay is a positively charged element, which means it attaches to negative elements. If it comes into contact with anything metallic, it becomes toxic. Use wooden or plastic utensils for all recipes containing bentonite, and if you're intending to make a toothpaste and you have metal fillings, use the alternative given on page 96.

Cocoa Butter An edible, ultra-hydrating vegetable fat that is derived from the cocoa bean, which also gives us chocolate.

Emulsifying Wax (Vegetable Derived) A non-toxic emulsifier used in cosmetics to produce lotions and creams.

Essential Fatty Acid An essential fat that the body can't manufacture itself. EFA deficiency can lead to kidney and liver damage, anaemia, eczema, inflammations of the skin and hair, scaling and more.

Essential Oil A concentrated liquid containing aroma compounds from plants. Essential oils are used mostly as a fragrance, but have benefits individual to the plant used.

Grapeseed Oil Extracted from the seeds of grapes, grapeseed oil has strong antibacterial and antioxidant properties.

Honey (Raw) Derived from sustainable producers it maintains the moisture level in the skin and has antiseptic and antibacterial properties. Best to use raw if you can find it so you're getting straight honey with no alterations or additions.

Jojoba Oil Extracted from the seeds of the jojoba plant, this waxy oil is similar in nature to our own sebum. It helps to lubricate and protect the skin.

Keratin A protein found in our hair, nails and skin and in the horns, hooves and claws of other mammals. Most commonly added to hair products to give strength and smoothness.

Macrobiotic Sea Salt This is made by the action of sun and wind on sea water.

Magnesium A naturally occurring salt used as a thickener, colouring or anticaking agent. Magnesium sulphate is often known as Epsom salts and is used to ease muscle tension and stress and to reduce certain seizures.

Peptides Shorter chains of amino acids combined to create proteins, these target wrinkles and aging of the skin.

Saponification The process of making a fatty acid into a salt by treating with an alkali; to saponify is to convert to soap.

Saponin A natural glycoside (sugar compound) that occurs in plants, such as sarsaparilla. It is mainly used as a foaming agent.

Shea Butter Derived from the fruit of the karate tree, shea butter is deeply moisturizing, softening and nourishing and leaves a protective film on the skin.

Tea tree oil A steam distilled from the leaves and flowers of the tea tree, this has strong antibacterial and antiseptic properties.

Vegetable Glycerine A thick, syrupy substance present in the fats and oils of vegetables. It helps to hydrate, soften and soothe the skin and assist in the retention of moisture.

Waxes (Beeswax, Soy Wax, Calendilla Wax) Obtained from animals, insects and plants though there are also mineral and synthetic waxes. Chemically, they are mostly a compound of various fatty acids, and are less greasy than fats or butters. To remove requires a solvent – the best is turpentine as it dissolves wax completely.

Zinc A chemical element (Zn), mostly used as a protective coating to other metals. Zinc is an essential element in the growth of many organisms, both plant and animal. A deficiency in zinc in humans has been found to stunt growth and contribute to anaemia.

Zinc Oxide A naturally occurring mineral, used as an antiseptic, astringent and in protective creams like sunblock.

HANDS
#ahelpinghand

When talking about essentials, where better to start than the part of our body we probably clean most often – our hands.

Back in high school I worked a few nights a week in a nursing home near my house. During my training nothing was stressed more than the need to wash your hands. Any bathroom in any hospital, nursing home or childcare centre will (or should) have a plaque detailing the correct way to lather up. As I'm all too aware of how important this is, I always carry my own hand sanitizer so I can keep my hands clean and nourished even if I'm in a hurry.

The problem I've found with commercial soaps and cleaners is that they all contain a little nasty called a surfactant (also known as detergent). These come in various guises, but they're designed to create the lather that removes bacteria; unfortunately, they're also insanely bad for your health. Like any detergent they usually come with a *Do Not Swallow* sign sitting right next to the *Keep Out of the Reach of Children* sticker. While it's quite normal to see warnings on products these days, if you can't swallow the contents, you really shouldn't be wearing them.

Skin is the body's largest organ and it behaves a little like a sponge. If you're lathering up your hands with all those harsh chemicals to keep them clean, your body is 'drinking' them in to your bloodstream. I'm sure you wouldn't pour hand wash into a glass and knock it back, or try to eat soap like a pastry (although when I was a kid, cursing usually came with having your mouth washed out with soap), but that's exactly what you're doing when you apply it to your skin. Like I said, if you can't eat it you can't wear it.

The recipes that follow are all-natural and edible (though I personally wouldn't recommend eating even these soaps – they're safe, but they'll taste disgusting!). Whether you're a soapie star, a hand-wash gal or a sensible sanitizer, make the switch to an all-natural version; and while they all moisturize as well as clean, I've included a couple of lotions to keep your hands 'handshake ready' at all times.

X

All-Natural Soap (Lye-Free)

Makes several bars
Shelf life: 12 months

3 pre-cut vegetable glycerine
   chunks (about 500g/1lb 2oz)
15 or more drops essential oil of
   choice (how much depends
   upon the strength of the scent)
Vegetable oil cooking spray

No bathroom would be complete without soap and making your own should be fun, not dangerous. However, most DIY soap-making recipes contain a little ingredient known as lye. Although it sounds harmless it's a chemical compound (known as sodium hydroxide) that is extremely toxic. It can burn the skin, cause blindness, is fatal if swallowed, and when mixed with heat is highly flammable. Problem is, real soap can't be made without it – it's impossible! This was what I found most frustrating when I first started to make my own products, but after a little trial and error, I came up with the alternative. It's not soap like you know soap, but it's pretty damn close.

Make a double boiler by placing a small glass bowl over a pan of simmering water. Allow the water to lap at the bowl, but not to flow over the edges of the pan. Add the glycerine chunks to the bowl and allow them to melt to a clear liquid.

Gently stir in your choice of essential oil (you can add more or less depending on how strong you like the smell – some essential oils may need up to 50 drops to smell really delicious, but do be mindful of the appropriate dilution for each oil; always read the safety label on the bottle).

Spray the soap mould (you can use a loaf tin if you don't have a mould) with the vegetable oil.

Pour the glycerine mixture into the mould and allow to cool and harden for about 3 hours or until completely solidified. Then pop out the soap with your fingers (use a knife to loosen the edges first, if necessary). If you used a loaf tin, then cut the soap into individual bars at whatever size you prefer.

---

*It's best not to stir the glycerine too much while it's melting, as you'll end up with soap that's cloudy. You can buy glycerine (and glycerine soap) online (see Directory, page 124).

*If you prefer a cloudy soap, by all means use soy or shea butter in place of the glycerine chunks.

Nourishing Hand Sanitizer

I've always had a love/hate relationship with hand sanitizers: they're too drying, too runny, too smelly, or too full of nasty chemicals to make them any better than germs. These days, however, I never leave home without some: one lives permanently in my handbag, and another in my car (just in case). Making your own is one of the best things you'll ever do (if for no other reason than buying them is uber pricey); you can control the ingredients, the scent, and the style. I like mine to dry and moisturize at the same time – not an easy thing to do.

Since making my own products, I've tried making sanitizers a hundred different ways, but this is still my favourite.

Makes about 250ml/9fl oz/1 cup
Shelf life: 2 months

225g/8oz aloe vera gel
6–8 drops tea tree essential oil
6–8 drops spearmint essential oil
30 drops grapeseed oil
¼ tsp vitamin E oil
2 tbsp rose water
4 tsp vodka

Place the aloe vera gel in a glass bowl and add the tea tree, spearmint and grapeseed oils, then stir in the vitamin E oil until everything is thoroughly combined. Stir in the rose water and vodka to loosen the mixture, then transfer to a squeezy cosmetics bottle or pump dispenser.

#everyonelovesaquickie The easiest hand sanitizer is a few drops of tea tree oil straight into your palms. Otherwise, use 1 tbsp aloe vera gel mixed with 1 tsp of alcohol (rubbing/isopropyl or vodka is fine). If you have a little bottle then use 1 part alcohol to 4 parts aloe vera.

Walnut Whip Hand Soap

One of my big gripes with soap/hand wash is that it completely dries out your skin: enter soap the whipped-up way. This recipe calls for silk peptides, which are a rich source of proteins that repair skin cells.

Walnut oil, like walnuts themselves, are a wonderful source of essential fatty acids, in this case omega-6 fats, which are great for healing eczema and psoriasis, sunburn, scalds and rashes, and they'll slow down skin-aging, too. What's not to love?! This recipe cleans and disinfects while also nourishing skin cells and repairing little blemishes.

Makes about 250g/9oz/1 cup
Shelf life: 4 months

40g/1½oz beeswax
100ml/3½fl oz/⅓ cup + 2 tbsp
    liquid Castile soap
90g/3¼oz shea butter
½ tsp silk peptides
2 tsp kaolin clay
1 tbsp walnut oil
10 drops carrot seed essential oil
25 drops petitgrain (orange leaf)
    essential oil

Make a double boiler by placing a glass bowl over a pan of simmering water. Allow the water to lap at the bowl, but not to flow over the edges of the pan. Add the beeswax to the bowl and heat gently until the wax has completely melted, then add the liquid soap and keep heating and stirring until the soap warms up and the wax remelts.

Once everything has melted, remove the bowl from the pan (take care – it will be hot) and use a hand-held electric whisk to bring everything together. It doesn't have to be completely smooth at this point, just fully combined.

Add the shea butter 1 tbsp at a time, whisking between each addition until eventually you get a lovely, fluffy mixture, like clouds of cream. Add the peptides, clay, walnut oil and both essential oils, then whip again to combine (or you can use a metal spoon if you prefer). Transfer to a clean glass jar or squeezy bottle and use as needed.

#everyonelovesaquickie The five-second version of a whipped soap is simply to combine 1 tsp each of bicarbonate of soda (baking soda) and shea butter and lather under warm water.

Lemon & Lime Hand Wash

I can't actually remember the last house I went into that didn't have hand wash in the bathroom; the theory being that it's more hygienic as germs can easily end up on soap and be passed to subsequent users. As I tend to use hand wash in place of soap, this is my go-to recipe for keeping clean. I keep a dispenser of this in both the kitchen and the bathroom, and seeing as citrus is such a popular smell, it's also my favourite for gifts.

Makes about 170ml/5½fl oz/
⅔ cup
Shelf life: 4 months

150ml/5fl oz/scant ⅔ cup liquid
Castile soap
15–20 drops lemon essential oil
20–30 drops lime essential oil

Put the liquid soap in a glass bowl. Combine 15 drops lemon and 20 drops lime essential oil in a separate glass bowl, then add the combined oils to the liquid soap a few drops at a time, giving the mixture a stir with a fork after each addition. Sniff every now and then and keep adding (combining more lemon and lime if you need to) until the soap smells delicious.

#everyonelovesaquickie The quickest hand wash is simply to use a fragranced liquid soap like Dr Bronner's liquid Castile soap. It comes in a variety of scents, or you can buy the scent-free version and add an essential oil of your choice, as above.

#everyonelovesaquickie Option 2 is to rinse your hands in vinegar (apple cider or white vinegar are the best). Vinegar is an antiseptic so no germs could survive a good dousing.

Forever Young Lavender Hand Lotion

The palms of your hands (and soles of your feet) are the only parts of the body that don't contain sebaceous glands, the glands that produce sebum. This means that they are prone to drying and aging more than anywhere else and means that a lotion for your digits is so important to keep them younger and healthier for longer.

Makes about 230g/8oz
Shelf life: 6 months

25g/1oz emulsifying wax
2 tsp avocado oil
2 tbsp safflower oil
1 tsp liquid vegetable glycerine
2 tsp Manuka honey or
   good-quality raw honey
10 drops lavender essential oil
2 drops German chamomile
   essential oil
4 drops neroli essential oil

Make a double boiler by placing a glass bowl over a pan of simmering water. Allow the water to lap at the bowl, but not to flow over the edges of the pan. Add the emulsifying wax along with the avocado and safflower carrier oils and heat gently until the wax has melted.

Meanwhile, boil a kettle of water, then measure out 145ml/4¾fl oz/ scant ⅔ cup into a measuring jug. Allow to cool to hand hot, then stir in the glycerine and honey until everything is liquid and combined.

Once the wax and carrier oils have melted, add the glycerine and honey mixture to the double boiler. Stir to combine and allow the mixture to heat up again over the simmering water for 1–2 minutes. Remove the bowl from the pan (take care – it will be hot), then use a hand whisk to whip it all up until smooth and thick. Allow the mixture to cool, then drop in the essential oils, stir to combine and transfer to a squeezy cosmetics bottle, or a foaming dispenser (see page 24).

#everyonelovesaquickie The easiest hand lotion is a spoonful of coconut oil or shea butter. Both will nourish the skin and replenish essential moisture to keep age spots at bay.

Honey & Vanilla Hand Lotion

When I was little my Nan used to tell me that you could always tell someone's age by their hands. Both the men and women in my life fret about face wrinkles, but our hands suffer more overuse and wear-and-tear than our faces. The hand-cream phenomenon has certainly picked up since I was young and making your own is the best way to ensure you're really keeping aging chemicals at bay.

Makes about 115g/4oz
Shelf life: 6 months

6g beeswax
6g emulsifying wax
2 tsp sweet almond oil
2 tsp marula oil
½ tsp liquid vegetable glycerine
1 tsp Manuka honey or
   good-quality raw honey
¼ tsp silk peptides
5 drops ginger essential oil
2 drops frankincense essential oil
15 drops vanilla essential oil

Make a double boiler by placing a glass bowl over a pan of simmering water. Allow the water to lap at the bowl, but not to flow over the edges of the pan. Add the beeswax, emulsifying wax and the almond and marula oils and heat gently until all the wax has melted.

Meanwhile, boil a kettle of water, then measure out 70ml/2¼fl oz/4½ tbsp into a measuring jug. Allow to cool to hand hot, then stir in the glycerine and honey until everything is liquid and combined, then add the silk peptides and stir to combine again.

Once the wax and carrier oils have melted, add the glycerine and honey mixture to the double boiler. Stir to combine and allow the mixture to heat up again over the simmering water for 1–2 minutes. Remove the bowl from the pan (take care – it will be hot), then use a hand whisk to whip it all up until smooth and thick. Allow the mixture to cool, then drop in the essential oils, stir to combine and transfer to a squeezy cosmetics bottle or a foaming dispenser (see page 24).

You don't have to use a foaming dispenser, this is just for convenience and to extend the shelf life. If you'd prefer to use a jar, please ensure it is glass or non-toxic plastic.

SHAMPOO
#thelatherheardroundtheworld

Ah, shampoo – the bane of my existence. I've lost count of how many varieties there are on the market these days – the big brands, the organic ones, the serums and masks and oils – it's a serious business! Unfortunately, a lot of the ingredients can cause the hair follicle to become damaged, which results in hair loss (which is what happened to me); not to mention, most are really not necessary in a shampoo.

In the modelling world, hair takes a beating; stylists apply – and reapply – sprays and gels, then there are the blow dries, straighteners, curling tongs and rollers, and that's without the dye jobs. At the end of my first round of Fashion Week, I returned home with a head of hair that resembled straw: not a pretty sight and it took several months to undo a lot of that damage. As women, our hair really is our crowning glory and back in the days when I worked in an office, one of my favourite things was seeing the array of hairstyles on display.

The recipes in this section are designed to clean the debris from the strands, while still nurturing and repairing the cells. They don't need to be used every day (in fact washing your hair that often is quite unnecessary), but they will work to keep your hair clean and healthy.

However, I do have a soft spot for shampoo; it was this very product that became the catalyst for my experiments, my products and my book. I'm most proud of these recipes as shampoo is no easy thing to create and it has taken years to get it just right (meaning I've spent months on end looking like a ball of grease).

If you've been a traditional hair-care user, then you're going to need a good two weeks for your body to adjust to this change. You may respond straightaway (some do) or you'll be a little extra oily for a bit as I was – and that's ok, too. Just as the skin produces oil, so too does the scalp, and when you stop stripping it out there's a little delay before the overproduction goes away and it regulates itself. Don't stress! Just keep your hair up, if you can, and try not to brush too often (or at all if you can avoid it – I actually haven't owned a hairbrush in years).

X

Wanted!
Naturally Beautiful Hair

When I was about nine there was a shampoo ad on television that featured a couple who had just been skiing. She walks into the cabin a mess, jumps in the shower and all of a sudden – beautiful hair. And, of course, who could forget the famous commercial where the girl's car breaks down and she goes to 'freshen up': all you hear from the bathroom is 'yes, yes, YES!' before she emerges with flowing, bouncing locks.

Most ads aren't designed to sell a product, they're designed to sell a lifestyle – a glamorous, beautiful lifestyle where the women are always happy and smiling with long limbs, designer clothes, flawless skin and, of course, healthy hair. Well here's my first big problem with shampoo ads: there's no such thing as 'healthy hair!' That's right: the hair itself (as in the strands you run your fingers through) is nothing more than dead tissue. It can't be healed because it was never alive to begin with, in fact the only thing most shampoo and conditioners do is add and subtract oils. Think of it like sending your clothes to a dry cleaner – they come back clean and pressed and beautiful, but the dry cleaner didn't make them 'healthy' as clothes are just as dead as hair. It's all an illusion!

My second big problem with commercial shampoo is that it caused all my hair to fall out. If you read the beginning of this book, then you'll know the story but if not, here are the facts – a few years ago my hair began falling out in clumps. It was devastating and unsightly and no one could tell me why or how to fix it. After months of stress, research and more stress, I found that one of the leading contributors to hair loss is shampoo and conditioner.

I'm sure all this is causing a quiet freak-out (it did for me, too) but there are options. First let's start with the dead hair – the strand is dead but the cell that holds it and causes it to grow is not. So it is in fact possible to have healthy hair if you're working at the right end. Your scalp needs all the nourishment while your strands really just need a few bits and bobs to clear away debris. Second, commercial products contain harsh chemicals and these can cause hair loss. Ergo, lose the dodgy chemicals and you'll have happy hair.

Grapefruit & Coconut Milk Shampoo

Makes about 150ml/5fl oz/
　　scant ⅔ cup
Shelf life: 4 weeks

60ml/2fl oz/¼ cup coconut milk,
　　preferably organic
80ml/2½fl oz/⅓ cup liquid Castile
　　soap
½ tsp sweet almond oil
20 drops grapefruit essential oil

This is my go-to shampoo recipe, and has had pride of place in my bathroom for years. Originally, I used plain liquid Castile soap (yes, even I enjoy an #everyonelovesaquickie now and then) and if you're short on time or want a 'no-brainer' that's what I recommend, but simply adding a few extra ingredients makes this not just a cleaner but a healer, too.

Coconut milk is extremely nourishing and full of essential nutrients that can help to heal damaged cells and speed up the regeneration process, while sweet almond oil is a good source of vitamin E, so helps create a barrier to protect the scalp from irritants and nasties.

Remember, your scalp will need a little time to adjust, but it will reward you in the long run with strong and beautiful hair.

Find a bottle with a secure lid – an old shampoo bottle will do, or alternatively you could use the foaming dispenser on page 24.

Making the shampoo couldn't be simpler. Pour the coconut milk, liquid soap and both oils into the bottle, secure the lid and shake vigorously to combine the ingredients. Use the shampoo just as you would shop-bought shampoo – lather into wet hair, then rinse; then apply and rinse again. You'll find that the shampoo separates if it's left to stand, so shake it again before each use (don't forget to make sure the lid is fastened before you shake!).

*If your hair is on the dry side, add an extra ½ tsp olive or sweet almond oil to the recipe to give your scalp extra hydration.

Hair Rescue Cypress & Rosemary Shampoo

This recipe is for when your hair needs repairing and nothing else will do. The phytokeratin provides protein that delves into the hair follicles and repairs root damage. If you're having hair-loss issues, I would definitely try this one (no more than three times a week). It includes petitgrain (also known as orange leaf) essential oil, which helps stimulate the follicles to promote growth.

Makes about 150ml/5fl oz/⅔ cup
Shelf life: 3 months

100ml/3½fl oz/⅓ cup + 2 tbsp liquid
   Castile soap
½ tsp arrowroot powder
1 tsp phytokeratin
1 tsp camellia oil
10 drops rosemary essential oil
15 drops cypress essential oil
5 drops petitgrain essential oil

Find a bottle with a secure lid – an old shampoo bottle will do, Pour the liquid soap into the bottle (use a funnel in the neck of the bottle if it makes it easier), then add the arrowroot and phytokeratin and all the essential oils. Pop on the lid, then shake the ingredients to fully combine. Wash your hair as with the shampoo on page 42, remembering to shake again (with the lid secure) before each use.

*While I usually recommend glass over plastic, if it's in your shower you're better with plastic. I myself have had a few slippery finger moments where the floor ends up covered in glass; it's not safe and not that easy to clean up.

#hisandherhacks

STOP STRIPPING YOUR HAIR

It's estimated that about 90 per cent of commercial shampoos contain sulphates, the foaming agent that can cause redness, dryness and irritation to the scalp. These shampoos also strip your hair of the natural oils that keep it healthy and vibrant. The scalp then overproduces oil to compensate, and you're left with a catch-22 situation where you end up having to wash (and strip) your hair more often. If you wash your hair every day, or if your scalp or hair is overly dry or greasy, then take note. There are several sulphate-free formulations on the market right now but the recipes on the right are so easy. You will also save a bundle.

Just be aware that it may take a week or two for your hair to acclimatize to this new regime, but once you are through the 'transitional phase', I promise you will never look back!

NORMAL SCALP/HAIR
Place 125ml/4fl oz/½ cup filtered water, 185ml/6fl oz/ ¾ cup liquid Castile soap, 1 tsp vitamin E oil and 1 tsp jojoba or olive oil in a bottle. Shake to combine and then shake again before each use.

OILY SCALP/HAIR
Place 70ml/2¼fl oz/¼ cup + 1 tbsp liquid Castile soap, ⅛ tsp peppermint oil, ¼ tsp tea tree oil and ⅛ tsp rosehip oil in a bottle and shake to combine. Then add 60ml/2fl oz/ ¼ cup filtered water and shake again. Give it another shake each time you use it.

DRY SCALP/HAIR
Place 60ml/2fl oz/¼ cup filtered water, 70ml/2¼fl oz/ ¼ cup + 1 tbsp liquid Castile soap and 185ml/6fl oz/¾ cup olive or jojoba oil in a bottle. Shake to combine and shake again before each use.

Revitalizing Citrus Shampoo

This one is for the ladies who love to colour. Dyeing your hair is a little like sending your scalp to boot camp, and not in a good way. Nonetheless, I know it's a joy to have different bases and streaks, and it is usually the first thing on a post break-up to-do list. If you're changing your hair as often as your underwear, your locks are going to need extra protection and a lot of soothing. These ingredients will restore the cells and keep them healthy even after all those toxins.

Makes about 150ml/5fl oz/ scant ⅔ cup
Shelf life: 2 months

100ml/3½fl oz/⅓ cup + 2 tbsp liquid Castile soap
2 tsp aloe vera powder
2 drops vanilla essential oil
5 drops cypress essential oil
10 drops lime essential oil
8 drops tangerine essential oil
4 drops lemon-scented eucalyptus essential oil
2 tsp dried calendula flowers

Put the Castile soap into a small glass bowl. Tip in the aloe vera powder and add all the essential oils, then mix everything together so that it is well combined and gorgeously fragrant without any lumps or streaks.

Place the calendula flowers in a pestle and mortar and grind to as fine a powder as you can – give your arm a thorough workout! If you have little pieces left over, don't worry – they'll rinse out when you rinse out the shampoo. Tip the flower powder into the oil mixture use a metal spoon to turn everything through so that the powder is evenly distributed. Transfer to a suitable container, such as the foaming dispenser on page 24, and use as the shampoo on page 42.

*If you don't fancy grinding the calendula flowers for an arm workout, make calendula-infused oil by filling a glass jar with the flowers (and leaves, if you can find them), pouring over light olive oil, sealing the jar and leaving the oil to infuse for up to 2 weeks. Drain and reserve the oil, discard the flowers (and leaves, if using) and, using the same oil, repeat with fresh flowers and leaves for extra intensity. To use, replace the calendula flowers in the shampoo recipe with 1 tsp of infused oil.

Cinnamon & Ginger Shampoo Bar

I love the smell of warming spices: ginger, cinnamon and nutmeg are like Christmas in spiced form. The smell and the taste of them is so soothing and comforting that I decided to create my own spice-scented soap. This makes the perfect gift and will leave you smelling as yummy as dessert (perfect for a first date).

Makes about 4 shampoo bars
Shelf life: 12 months

400g/14oz vegetable glycerine melt-and-pour soap base, cut into chunks
2 tsp ground cinnamon
1 tsp ground nutmeg
2 tbsp cinnamon leaf essential oil
5 drops ginger essential oil
2 tsp white kaolin (China) clay
170g/6oz coconut cream

Make a double boiler by placing a large glass bowl over a large pan of simmering water. Allow the water to lap at the bowl, but not to flow over the edges of the pan. Add the pieces of soap base and heat gently until the soap pieces have melted.

Meanwhile combine the ground cinnamon and nutmeg in a small bowl.

Once the soap pieces have melted, remove the bowl from the pan (take care, the bowl will be hot) and add the essential oils and clay; stir to combine. Remove half the mixture into a separate, clean bowl. Stir the cinnamon and nutmeg mixture into one half, and the coconut cream into the other.

Using a fairly deep, rectangular soap mould, pour in a layer of milky shampoo mixture, then a layer of cinnamon shampoo mixture. (You can use a small, straight-sided loaf tin if you don't have a soap mould.) Add another layer of milky mixture, then finish with a layer of cinnamon. Repeat in separate moulds, if necessary, until you have used all the mixture.

Leave the shampoo bars to solidify for 1–2 days, then remove from the mould and slice each into smaller pieces, so that you can see the stripy layers, if you like. To use, lather the shampoo bar in your hands with hot water before applying to your hair and then use like a normal liquid shampoo.

Volumizing Dry Shampoo

I'm not always a fan of washing my hair; sometimes I'm busy, tired, running late or simply can't be bothered, so dry shampoo is one of the 'must-haves' in my beauty arsenal. This is a deluxe version, but if you're an #everyonelovesaquickie gal, then just mix equal parts arrowroot powder and a powder that matches your hair colour. Bing, bang, boom, you're done!

Makes about 60g/2¼oz
Shelf life: 4 months

1 tbsp arrowroot powder or
   cornstarch
1 tbsp bicarbonate
   of soda
2 tsp zinc oxide
1 tbsp cinnamon for red hair or
   1 tbsp unsweetened cocoa
   powder for brown hair (optional
   – if you are fair, add neither!)
10 drops lemon-scented
   eucalyptus essential oil, or
   cedarwood essential oil, or
   essential oil of choice

Place the arrowroot or cornstarch powder, bicarbonate of soda and zinc oxide in a glass bowl and stir to combine. Use a fork and the back of a spoon to press out and break down any lumpy bits.

Add your chosen essential oil a few drops at a time, stirring and pressing out any new lumps as you go. Stop adding the oils when the powder smells delicious.

Then, little by little add the cinnamon or cocoa powder (or you can combine the two if you have auburn hair – feel free to experiment) until you get something that perfectly matches your locks. Again, press out any lumps and combine everything together fully. Press the powder through a fine sieve into a separate, clean bowl if it helps.

Pour the finished shampoo into an airtight glass jar. To use, take a large make-up brush and dab on the powder at the roots of your hair, dividing your hair into sections as necessary. When you've got good coverage, style as desired.

How to Stretch Out Your Washes

Washing too often is bad for your hair, but you can actually train it to need cleaning less frequently. In fact, leaving your hair for six weeks with no products will return it to its natural state and it will never need washing again. I did try this but I couldn't survive more than two weeks with dirty, DIRTY, hair so instead I came up with a system for getting the most out of each wash.

MOVE OVER TO NATURAL SHAMPOO
If you haven't already (what's stopping you?), try one of the recipes in this section or if you're in a hurry, check out the #hisandherhacks on page 44. Just give your hair a couple of weeks to acclimatize before you start stretching out your washes.

FORGET THE CONDITIONER
I know it feels weird to forego conditioner, but trust me, it's really not necessary if you're using a natural shampoo. Hold off until you've lengthened the time between washes and then you can start using it again, albeit occasionally (I find once a week is enough).

TAKE IT DAY BY DAY
Lengthen the time before washes one extra day at a time. I got down to washing once every three or four days quite quickly, but it took a few months before I could last for six or seven days.

LEAVE THE COMB ALONE
If you can resist, stop combing or brushing your hair in the morning – it can make your hair look and feel greasy. Comb out any your tangles before bed instead and if your hair's long enough you could braid it as well. Then just smooth out with your fingers in the morning.

STYLE IT UP
On greasier days go with a top-knot or slicked back ponytail if you have long hair, or if you have short hair try experimenting with clips, an Alice band or even a headscarf for the rockabilly look.

WHIP UP SOME DRY SHAMPOO
Follow the recipe opposite to assist with any greasy days when you're past the halfway point in your cycle.

HAIR RINSES

#rinseandrepeat

Cuticle care isn't just important for your nails, people! Under a microscope, a strand of your hair appears to be covered with scales or roof tiles – this is the protective layer of cuticles. When these are healthy, the layers lie flat and make your hair look smooth and shiny, but when the cuticles become damaged, the hair starts to look limp and dull.

Shampooing opens the layers, so a good rinse will remove the build-up of hair products and toxins; close the cuticles so your hair slides easily, leaving you with fewer tangles; improve circulation to your scalp; maintain the pH balance (just like on your face) and protect against hair loss, dandruff, dry scalp and more. Think of a rinse as toner for your hair; in the same way a toner for your face helps protect and restore the skin, so does a rinse. It's all part of the three-step system for healthy hair and it's a vital one. I'll admit I don't always rinse every time I wash, I don't even condition and to be fair when you're using an all-natural shampoo loaded with nutrients, you don't really need to, but that doesn't mean you can't. When it comes to your hair, more is definitely more, and if you want your crowning glory to be the best it can be then I recommend using a rinse at least once a week after shampooing (Sunday is my preferred day) and skip the conditioner.

If your hair is greasy after rinsing (it depends on your hair type), treat your hair only from the middle to the ends of the strands, not the roots – this way, you'll have super-shiny, commercial-ready hair.

X

Aromatic Vinegar Hair Rinse

Makes about 500ml/17fl oz/2 cups
Shelf life: 18 months

100ml/3½fl oz/⅓ cup + 2 tbsp
    apple cider vinegar
¼ tsp xantham gum
½ tsp sulphated castor bean oil
    (sometimes called turkey red oil)
8 drops myrtle essential oil
10 drops tea tree essential oil
4 drops elemi essential oil
½ tsp silk peptides
½ tsp phytokeratin

This is my number-one favourite rinse and I've been using it every Sunday for over two years. Packed with amino acids (the chains in protein), it not only makes my hair aesthetically beautiful, but protects all the little strands from damage. I mentioned before that the hair strands are dead, but that doesn't mean they need to decay and become vegetables. If you're a newbie to rinses, this is definitely the one I recommend. If you're short on time, your #everyonelovesaquickie version is just to use diluted apple cider vinegar (start with a ratio of one part vinegar to four parts water, and experiment until you find a balance that suits you).

Boil a kettle of water and leave to cool, then measure out 400ml/14fl oz/ 1½ cups + 2 tbsp into a measuring jug.

Find a bottle with a secure lid – an old shampoo bottle will do. Pour in the apple cider vinegar, using a funnel if it makes it easier.

Pour 60ml/2fl oz/¼ cup of the water into a medium-sized measuring jug, then sprinkle over the xantham gum. Using a small hand whisk or a fork, combine the gum and the water. Keep whisking as you pour in the castor bean oil. Add the essential oils one at a time and continue to whisk until the mixture turns opaque and creamy. (The castor bean oil acts as an emollient, allowing the oils and water to combine fully.)

Again using a funnel if it helps you, pour the creamy essential oil mixture into the bottle with the apple cider vinegar, then add the silk peptides and phytokeratin. Close the lid on the bottle and give the mixture a shake. Open the bottle again and add the remaining cooled, once-boiled water. Replace the lid and shake again until the hair rinse is fully combined.

Lavender Tea & Citrus Hair Rinse

If vinegar is one way to rinse your hair, then lemon juice is the other as they function quite similarly. Both acidic, when ingested they become alkaline; they're also antiviral, antifungal and antiseptic and create a glossy shine in the hair. Vinegar does smell quite putrid if you ask me, so if you can't take the scent, then lemon juice is your next-best thing, and just like vinegar it can be used diluted with a little water (or neat if you prefer) as an #everyonelovesaquickie. I like to use straight lemon juice when I'm travelling as room service will always have fresh lemons if I haven't had time to whip to the market.

Makes about 250ml/9fl oz/1 cup
Shelf life: 6 months

2 tbsp lavender flowers
1 tsp Manuka honey, or
    good-quality raw honey
Juice of ½ a lemon
10 drops eucalyptus essential oil
5 drops German chamomile
    essential oil
4 drops frankincense essential oil

Start by making a lavender infusion – just like making a cup of lavender tea. Place the lavender flowers in a large mug and pour over 250ml/9fl oz/ 1 cup just-boiled water. Allow the water to infuse for 5–10 minutes. Use a tea strainer to strain the infused water into a separate mug. Discard the used flowers and reserve the infusion.

Put the honey into a small glass bowl and add the tea, then stir it through to combine thoroughly. Add the lemon juice and essential oils and stir again to make sure everything is properly mixed together. Transfer to a suitable bottle (plastic is better for the shower).

HAIR
CONDITIONERS
#conditionlikeapro

A few years ago a hairstylist and friend taught me a little known secret to having beautiful (TV-ad worthy) hair: use your conditioner first. Seems a little odd, but the theory is that you never quite rinse your hair thoroughly enough after you condition, leaving a build-up of residue that causes it to look lacklustre and flat. He assured me that reversing the order would be the best thing I'd ever do for my locks and so I took up his week-long challenge.

The method itself is simple: wet your hair, then work in your favourite conditioner, focusing on the ends and using a small amount on the roots. Leave for five minutes, then rinse thoroughly. Follow with shampoo, rinse, and repeat with a second round of shampoo. I won't lie, having used conditioner post shampoo all my life, switching the order just felt wrong, plus slathering conditioner onto already dirty hair had me stressing I'd spend the day looking like a grease mop. I persevered, thankfully, and by the end of the seven days my hair was thicker, softer, shinier and easier to manage. It's one of the best pieces of advice I've ever been given and my hair still gets the same results every time.

I'm a little sneaky with adding a rinse between the first and second round of shampooing, but I didn't use a rinse back then and my hair still had amazing results, so if you're game I definitely recommend trying the reverse order for a week.

These days I use a conditioner only once a week as my shampoo does it all, but you can use one as often as you shampoo or every other time, whatever you find gives you the best results.

X

Coconut & Almond Conditioning Balm

This was my go-to conditioner for such a long time because it's super easy to make and I do, of course, love all things coconut. The method that worked best for me was to massage the equivalent of ½ tsp into my scalp and ½ tbsp into the ends of my hair; if your hair is short then just a little into the scalp is plenty. Start small and build up the amount you use, as this natural version will shock your system if you've always used traditional conditioners in the past. The results, though, are pretty impressive and the smell is even better. Call it a little touch of Tahiti!

Makes about 250g/9oz
Shelf life: 12 months

150g/9oz coconut oil
100ml/3½fl oz/⅓ cup + 2 tbsp
    sweet almond oil
1 tsp Australian sandalwood
    essential oil
1 tsp jojoba oil
3 drops lavender essential oil
2 drops Roman chamomile
    essential oil

Make a double boiler by placing a large glass bowl over a large pan of simmering water. Allow the water to lap at the bowl, but not to flow over the edges of the pan. Add the coconut oil and heat gently until melted. Remove the bowl from the pan (take care – it will be hot), then allow the coconut oil to cool a little, but not so much that it resolidifies.

Add the sweet almond oil to the bowl with the melted coconut oil and stir to combine. Add the sandalwood, jojoba, lavender and Roman chamomile essential oils and stir again until the mixture is fully combined.

Transfer the mixture to a suitable airtight container, fix on the lid, then place in the refrigerator for 20–30 minutes, until the balm has solidified. You can store the balm at room temperature in the container until you need it. To use, rub a little balm between the palms of your hands and run your hands through your hair when wet. Rinse well and leave to air dry if possible.

#everyonelovesaquickie Straight coconut oil is fine to use as a conditioner on its own, if you don't have time to whip up something more elaborate.

Sweet Basil & Orange Conditioner

Makes about 200ml/7fl oz/
    scant 1 cup
Shelf life: 6 months

1 tsp marshmallow root
40g/1½oz flax seeds
¼ tsp liquid vegetable glycerine
1 tsp arrowroot powder
½ tsp phytokeratin
5g beeswax
5g emulsifying wax
1 tbsp grapeseed oil
5 drops sweet basil or basil
    essential oil
2 tsp geranium essential oil
2 drops rosemary essential oil
15 drops sandalwood essential oil
15 drops sweet orange essential
    oil

Marshmallow root (and no I don't mean the little fluffies you get in your hot chocolate) was originally used as a medicine because it's highly antiseptic. It's great for everything from sore throats to sore scalps (I'm talking dandruff), plus it creates slip, which is the separation of the hair strands so there are no tangles. Flax is rich in essential fatty acids, especially omega-3 fats, that will nourish your hair and scalp, and strengthen your hair keeping it thick, glossy and smooth.

Place the marshmallow root and flax seeds in a large, heatproof bowl and pour over 200ml/7fl oz/scant 1 cup boiling water. Leave to infuse for 15 minutes, then place the bowl over a large pan of simmering water to make a double boiler. Allow the water to lap at the bowl, but not to flow over the edges of the pan. Allow the flax and marshmallow-root mixture to cook away in the double boiler for about 5 minutes until it starts to thicken and turn into a gel. Quickly remove the bowl from the pan (take care – it will be hot) and pour the gel-like mixture through a sieve to strain it into a clean jar – the mixture will thicken further as it cools, so work quickly otherwise it will be hard to pass through the sieve. Leave to cool and thicken up in the jar. Once the gel has cooled, stir in the glycerine, arrowroot powder and phytokeratin until combined.

Make a second double boiler using a clean glass bowl. Put the beeswax and emulsifying wax into the bowl and warm over the simmering water until melted. Meanwhile, combine all the essential oils in a separate glass bowl.

Add the gel mixture to the double boiler and stir it through the melted wax. Remove the bowl from the heat (take care – it will be hot) and use a hand whisk to mix together until everything turns thick and creamy. Stir in the combined essential oils. Store in a squeezy plastic cosmetics tube or glass foaming dispenser (see page 24).

*You should need only about a walnut-sized amount of this, mixed in your hands with the shower water. Then just apply to your hair and rinse thoroughly.

*You can use the marshmallow root and flax seed gel as a hair gel, if you like. Simply add a few drops of your favourite essential oil and you're done!

HAIR MASKS

#thesecret

If only every day was a great hair day! Those occasions when your hair is extra-swishy and just falls beautifully in to place seem all too rare and random. But rather than leaving it to chance, I now give my hair a weekly treat to make those good hair days come around more often. This means nourishing the scalp and hair roots with a homemade hair mask.

Now I'm not a fan of buying ready-made hair masks and putting all those toxins directly into my scalp; one, they're pricey, and two, I know I can make them myself. But before I give you a whole bunch of recipes, here's what you need to know.

Mask once a week, even if you think your hair is healthy. Masking is all about taking good care of the scalp.

The best time to apply your mask is pre-shower, or if you prefer, you can apply the hair mask to your dry hair before bed, leave it on overnight and wash it off in the morning.

Wash the mask off thoroughly with shampoo, otherwise you'll end up with a greasy helmet!

All masks work differently, depending on the ingredients you use, so make sure you follow the instructions for your chosen mask.

The following recipes are straight from the fridge: they're easy, nourishing and full of goodness. I pick depending on what I think my hair needs at that time. If you are going to sleep in them (and you can with all of them), then I would suggest a towel over your pillow and wrapping your head in clingfilm or a shower cap or you'll wake up with a mushy bed.

X

Hair Masks
#everyonelovesaquickie

Tropical FOR EXTRA STRENGTH
Blend 2 over-ripe bananas until smooth. Add 1 tbsp sweet almond oil,
1 tbsp apricot kernel oil and 1 tbsp Manuka (or other good-quality) honey
and blend again. Apply to dry hair, leave for 10 minutes, then rinse.

Papaya TO HEAL SPLIT ENDS
Blend ½ a ripe papaya with 1 tbsp olive oil and 125ml/4fl oz/½ cup natural
yogurt until smooth. Apply to dry hair. Leave for 20–30 minutes, then rinse.

Strawberry FOR SUPER-SHINE
Blend 10–12 strawberries with 1 tbsp coconut oil and 1 tbsp aloe vera gel.
Apply to dry hair and leave for 15–20 minutes. Rinse well.

Pumpkin FOR ADDED VOLUME
Blend 2 cups cooked and chopped pumpkin with 1 tbsp coconut oil,
1 tbsp honey and 1 tbsp natural yogurt. Apply to damp hair and cover with
a shower cap. Leave for 15 minutes and rinse well.

Yo-cado FOR EXTRA-SOFT LOCKS
Blend the flesh of 1 avocado with 125ml/4fl oz/½ cup natural yogurt and
1 tbsp each of argan oil and walnut oil. Apply to damp hair and leave for
10 minutes, then rinse well.

Egghead FOR SHINE, CELL REPAIR AND BOUNCE
Beat 1 large egg in a bowl. Add 250ml/9fl oz/1 cup milk and 2 tbsp olive oil to
the egg and mix well. Add a squeeze of lemon and mix again. Apply to dry or
damp hair. Leave for 15 minutes, then rinse well.

Colour Enhancers
BRUNETTES: Rinse with ground coffee and warm water.
REDHEADS: Rinse with cranberry juice and warm water.
BLONDES: Rinse with a glass of Champagne.

HAIR STYLING

#styleisinthehair

One of my favourite TV shows is *Damages* with Glenn Close and Rose Byrne. It's a great show, but in season two my favourite thing was how many times Rose's character changed her hair style. I'll admit I was obsessed and took to experimenting with as many of the dos as I could.

These days at home I almost never put styling products through my hair, in fact I don't even own a hairbrush – I just let my hair dry naturally and run my fingers through it a few times to tame any tangles. At work, however, my hair has seen some shockers: curling, teasing, straightening, you name it. It's not just the fashion world that is so fastidious with hair: back in my ballet days I wore a bun so tight, with thousands of bobby pins and so much gel and spray to keep everything in place, while I pirouetted and jumped around the stage.

Styling products can be some of the most overdosed chemical concoctions of all the cosmetics and there have been dozens of studies linking sprays to the hole in the ozone layer (not to mention the fact that they stink).

Fortunately, there are endless options for making your own. For the #everyonelovesaquickie fans: place 1 tbsp Epsom salts and ½ tbsp jojoba oil in a spray bottle, fill with water, shake and – hey presto – all-natural hair spray!

Citrus Hair Gel

I'll admit I'm not much of a gel user these days, but my former partner (and best mate) certainly was; I would go as far as to say he was obsessed with his hair. Aside from the irritation of getting glue-like hands every time I touched his head or having my pillow cases covered in muck, his hair was in terrible condition (yes, hair gel can also cause hair loss). I made this recipe for him and all my male friends (the ones with hair) who like to look styled all day.

Makes about 250ml/9fl oz/1 cup
Shelf life: 4 weeks

½ tbsp unflavoured gelatine
8 drops mandarin essential oil
2 drops lemon essential oil

Pour 100ml/3½fl oz/⅓ cup + 2 tbsp hot but not boiling water into a bowl and sprinkle over the gelatine powder. Stir until the gelatine has all dissolved, then top up with 150ml /5fl oz/scant ⅔ cup cold water. Refrigerate for 3 hours, until set. Remove from the fridge, stir in the essential oils and transfer to a suitable container. Use as necessary.

Botanical Texturizing Spray

I love this spray for giving me some volume when my hair is feeling a little flat. It smells amazing and is really designed for texture as opposed to hold.

Makes about 250ml/9fl oz/1 cup
Shelf life: 3 months

1 tbsp fine sea salt
1 tbsp caster sugar
2 tsp jojoba oil
5 drops rosemary essential oil
5 drops lemon-scented
  eucalyptus essential oil
1 tsp unflavoured vodka (optional)

Place the salt and sugar in a glass bowl and pour over 250ml/9fl oz/1 cup hot once-boiled, slightly cooled water. Give the mixture a good stir until the salt and sugar are fully dissolved in the water.

Allow to cool to room temperature, then add the jojoba oil, the essential oils, and the vodka, if using (the alcohol will help to prevent the spray sticking in your hair). Give the mixture a good stir until fully combined, then transfer to a plastic spray bottle. Shake before each use.

Orange & Cardamom Hair Spray

For the last few months I've been sporting a very short (shaved undercut) hairdo, which thankfully is growing out – it was, after all, for work. Having short hair usually means waking up in the morning looking like Johnny Bravo and a cockatoo had a baby, which is why I love DIY hair spray. This one offers a quick and easy way to style unmanageable hair, whether long or short – plus no harmful chemicals floating up into the air.

Makes about 250ml/9fl oz/1 cup
Shelf life: 3 months

2 tbsp caster sugar
½ tsp sea salt
1 tsp aloe vera gel
½ tsp coconut oil, melted
1 tbsp freshly pressed orange juice
3 drops cardamom essential oil

Place the sugar and salt into a small bowl and pour over 250ml/9fl oz/ 1 cup once-boiled, slightly cooled water. Stir the water until the sugar and salt have dissolved. Add the aloe vera gel, melted coconut oil, orange juice and essential oil and stir to fully combine. Transfer the mixture to a plastic spray bottle. Store at warm room temperature, to prevent the coconut oil from re-solidifying. Shake before each use.

#hisandherhacks

DANDRUFF BE GONE... WITH COCONUT OIL?

Dandruff is an incredibly common problem and those little white flakes are just so annoyingly persistent.

Shampooing too often actually encourages dandruff as it strips the hair of its natural oils, but if you've switched to an all-natural shampoo and are washing your hair less frequently then you're already on the right track.

One of the best and easiest home remedies I've found to treat dandruff is good old coconut oil. It's naturally antifungal so combats the yeast-like fungus in the scalp that dandruff sufferers are sensitive to. Plus it works as a moisturizer for your scalp: win-win.

Place 1-2 tbsp of warmed coconut oil (depending on hair length) in a small bowl. Gradually massage into your scalp with your fingertips, then finger-comb the oil through to the tips of your hair. Don a shower cap and leave the oil to do its thing for a good thirty minutes - or even overnight if it's convenient. Rinse your hair and wash with natural shampoo.

THE BODY BEAUTIFUL

#headtotoe

Every day your body works tirelessly to protect you: keeping you healthy, your heart pumping, lungs breathing, cells rebuilding and that's without combating any illness. I liken caring for your body to caring for a small child – you feed it nourishing foods, bathe it, nurture it and treat it with so much love. The Body Beautiful is a collection of recipes for showing your life's vessel some much needed TLC and to give it a little assistance in the areas where every now and then it probably struggles.

Our bodies lose thousands of skin cells a year and sometimes they can get stuck on our skin along with other debris, so we need a little scrub to help the new skin to breathe. Sometimes our bodies are so busy taking care of us they forget to keep the skin cells hydrated, so we need to give our limbs some extra nourishment. Sometimes we are stressed or exercising heavily and we want to feel clean and deodorized so we need a good antiperspirant (also useful on a daily basis to keep pongs at bay). Sometimes we need to help keep our feet healthy and soothe our sunburnt skin; and sometimes we, and our bodies, just need some rest and relaxation.

This section is split into all those little areas that need some extra loving. From relaxing bath salts all the way to body butter, these recipes will have you feeling (and smelling) good as new.

My bathroom is full of these concoctions and I change scents based on my mood; I like to keep a few different flavours, smells and variations so that I'm always covered for choice. Think of these as a way to thank your body for everything it does for you each and every day and have fun experimenting with your own essential oils and colours so you can create your own personalized favourites.

X

Hydrating Bath Milk

Much like the Muscle Relief Bath Salts (see page 72), this bath milk is great for relieving fluid retention. Great news, of course, but sometimes I also want a bath that makes me feel like I'm at a spa. This recipe is hydrating and nourishing and great for relaxing tired muscles and irritated skin. Lavender promotes relaxation and eases anxiety.

Makes about 500ml/17fl oz/
   2 cups
Shelf life: 24 hours

2 tbsp coconut oil
15 drops lavender essential oil
15g/½oz/¼ cup lavender buds
280g/10oz/1 cup Epsom salts
100g/3½oz/½ cup bicarbonate
   of soda (baking soda)
125ml/4fl oz/½ cup full cream milk

Make a double boiler by placing a large glass bowl over a large pan of simmering water. Allow the water to lap at the bowl, but not to flow over the edges of the pan. Add the coconut oil and heat gently until melted. Remove the bowl from the pan (take care – it will be hot), then allow the coconut oil to cool a little, but not so much that it resolidifies.

Place all the remaining ingredients in the bowl with coconut oil and mix together to fully combine. Transfer to a plastic cosmetics bottle or use immediately poured into your bath water, agitating the water with your hand as the bath runs. Luxuriate in the milk for 20 minutes to rehydrate and soothe.

Muscle Relief Bath Salts

My standard bathtime ritual, which I indulge in at least once a week, involves some candles, a little classical music and a soothing salt-based concoction added to the water. I was first introduced to Epsom salts by a fellow model on a lingerie shoot. Her secret was to bathe the night before in these magical crystals to help relieve any water retention – it should be noted she looked incredible! Epsom salts have a natural way of flushing excess toxins and helping you de-bloat (always a good thing if you ask me). They do work on their own (#everyonelovesaquickie), but I've found a few extra ingredients really up the ante.

Makes about 750ml/26fl oz/3 cups
Shelf life: 24 months

150g/3½oz/½ cup Celtic sea salt
  or Himalayan pink salt
400g/10oz/1 cup Epsom salts
200g/7oz/1 cup bicarbonate of
  soda (baking soda)
5 drops vetiver essential oil
  (optional)
15 drops sweet orange essential oil

Place the sea salt, Epsom salts and bicarbonate of soda in a bowl and stir thoroughly to fully combine. Add the vetiver essential oil, if using, and the sweet orange and stir again, until the oils are mixed through. Transfer to an airtight container. To use, place 1–2 tbsp of the salts in your bathwater.

Calming Bedtime Bubble Bath

This is the bubble bath I reach for when I feel overtired and in need of a nurturing bath to take me to the land of nod. Sometimes simple is best when your mind is racing and you can't settle. Be kind to yourself and remember – tomorrow is another day!

Makes about 330ml/11¼fl oz/
   1⅓ cups
Shelf life: 3 months

250ml/9fl oz/1 cup liquid Castile
   soap (such as Dr Bronner's)
80ml/2½fl oz/⅓ cup sweet almond
   oil
1 tsp nutmeg essential oil
1 tsp lavender essential oil
1 tbsp raw honey

Place the soap, the sweet almond oil and both essential oils in a clean glass bowl or large measuring jug and stir gently to fully combine, taking care not to froth up the ingredients. Drizzle in the honey, stirring gently as you go until it is fully mixed in. Transfer the mixture into a plastic bottle with tight-fitting lid. To use, pour under running water and froth up using your hand as the bath fills.

Lavender & Rose Body Conditioner

Makes about 300g/10½oz
Shelf life: 2 months

1 tbsp dried lavender flowers
   or rose buds
100g/3½oz shea butter
40g/1½oz coconut oil
1 tbsp beeswax
1 tbsp emulsifying wax
2 tbsp aloe vera gel
5 drops neroli essential oil
2 drops rose otto essential oil
   or 15 drops rose geranium
   essential oil

Body conditioners are a relatively new addition to the beauty world, the premise being that you apply them in the shower and rinse as you would with a hair conditioner. They're designed to soothe, provide the skin with essential moisture, and remove the need to use a lotion or body butter post shower. Personally, I am a lotion girl and enjoy taking that extra time in the morning to really nourish my skin, but if you're busy and you just want something that's hassle-free, a body conditioner is a great idea. This recipe is loaded with essential nutrients that will really penetrate the epidermis (the uppermost layer of skin) and rejuvenate the cells throughout.

Boil a kettle of fresh water. Place the lavender flowers or rose buds in a cup and pour over the once-boiled water, as if you were making a cup of tea. Leave the flowers to infuse for 15–20 minutes, then strain the liquid into a clean cup using a tea strainer to catch the flowers. Discard the flowers and allow the infusion to cool.

Make a double boiler by placing a glass bowl over a pan of simmering water. Allow the water to lap at the bowl, but not to flow over the edges of the pan. Add the shea butter, coconut oil, beeswax and emulsifying wax to the bowl and allow the ingredients to melt together. Give them a stir, then remove the bowl (take care – it will be hot) from the pan. Allow the mixture to cool, then place in the fridge for 15–20 minutes until it becomes soft set. Using an electric hand whisk, whip into a thick cream. Add the aloe vera gel and both essential oils and whip again. Finally, add 1 tbsp of the lavender infusion and whip again. Keep adding the infusion a tablespoon at a time, until you reach your desired consistency.

Transfer the lotion into a plastic cosmetics bottle. To use, apply liberally working into your skin to moisturize, then rinse off.

---

*If you suffer from arthritis or muscle aches and pains, try substituting the lavender or rose infusion with an infusion of goji berries. These have anti-inflammatory properties that help ease sore joints and muscles.

*Rose otto essential oil can be very expensive. Rose geranium has similar properties, but you'll need more of it to scent your body conditioner.

Feel Good Bath Tablets

I often make these for gifts as they're just so pretty – they look like little cupcakes. I love the thought and effort behind preparing something for a special someone, but then again, why not extend that love and affection to yourself, too? You will need some silicone moulds in whatever shape takes your fancy – I like to use star moulds the size of a large cupcake.

Makes 6 tablets
Shelf life: 6 months

1½ tbsp dried lavender flowers, and 3 tbsp dried chamomile flowers **or** 1½ tbsp dried linden (lime) flowers and 3 tbsp dried passionflower, plus extra for sprinkling
600g/1lb 5oz/3 cups bicarbonate of soda (baking soda)
18–24 drops essential oil (choose from the list below)

Soothing Essential Oils

Ylang ylang Soothing, sensual, calming.
Damiana Restorative, warming, pick-me-up.
Sweet marjoram Calming, nurturing, reassuring.
Nutmeg Strengthening, hopeful, positive.
Lime Energizing, refreshing, uplifting.
Melissa Cooling, relaxing, gentle.
Eucalyptus Clarifying.

Boil a kettle of fresh water and allow to cool completely. Preheat the oven to 180°C/350°F/Gas 4.

Place your chosen combination of dried flowers in a pestle and mortar and work the flowers until you have a fairly even, coarse powder. Tip the ground flowers into a small glass bowl and add 450g/1lb/3 cups bicarbonate of soda. Give the dry ingredients a good stir to combine.

Add the once-boiled cooled water a little at a time, stirring after each addition, until you have a thick paste. Spoon the paste evenly into a 6-hole silicone cupcake mould, then sprinkle each with a few extra whole dried flowers (press them into the top of the paste so that they hold firm once baked) and equal amounts of the remaining bicarbonate of soda (you need quite a thick layer of bicarbonate powder on top, as this stops the tablets discolouring during baking).

Bake the tablets in the preheated oven for 15–20 minutes, then remove and allow to cool. Once the tablets are completely cooled, remove them from the mould onto a wire rack, tap off the excess bicarbonate of soda, and place 3–4 drops of your chosen essential oil(s) onto the top of each one. Leave for 5 minutes to allow the essential oils to properly soak into the tablets, then transfer to an airtight container or a jar with a lid to store. To use, simply drop a tablet into the water as you run the bath.

Sensual Body Wash

Honey is so restorative and nourishing while also being antibacterial and antiseptic, so it's a valuable addition in a body wash. This is one of the first recipes I ever made. I love the flowery smell of this version (ylang ylang and vanilla, and choc-mint and grapefruit are my other favourites), but take out my essential oil choices and you have the perfect base for creating your own scent combos, and so your own favourite. I tend to have about three bottles of this body wash going at any one time, each with a different scent.

Makes about 200ml/7fl oz/
  ¾ cup + 2 tbsp
Shelf life: 3 months

125ml/4fl oz/½ cup liquid
  Castile soap
2 tbsp extra-virgin olive oil
1 tbsp apricot kernel oil
60ml/2fl oz/¼ cup raw honey
40 drops neroli essential oil
10 drops jasmine absolute
  essential oil

Place all the ingredients in your desired bottle (you could use a foaming dispenser for this; see page 24), and shake to combine. Shake again before each use.

---

*Jasmine absolute has mild aphrodisiac properties, making this a perfect body wash if you're preparing for a hot date.

Jojoba & Peppermint Foot Scrub

My soles are constantly taking a beating in impossible footwear, plus I go running most days which puts even more pressure on my feet. When I'm taking my bath, I scrub away the stresses of the week with this minty potion.

Makes about 120ml/4fl oz/½ cup
Shelf life: 3 months

6 fresh mint leaves, finely chopped
120g/4oz/½ cup sea salt (coarse
   or fine, according to preference)
16 drops peppermint essential oil
4 drops tea tree essential oil
4 tbsp jojoba oil

Place all the ingredients in a small bowl and stir to combine. Transfer to an airtight container and use as necessary.

*This, like most scrubs, makes a great gift – particularly as it's not something you'd buy for yourself. If I've received a last-minute invitation somewhere, I'll whip up a batch of this and put it in a glass jar with a green ribbon and a little 'how-to' card.

Orange & Pomegranate Body Scrub

As someone who exercises a lot, my skin can feel a little grimy and sweat can easily get stuck in the pores, so I use a body scrub a few times a week to slough away dead skin and give me an extra-good clean.

Makes about 500ml/17fl oz/2 cups
Shelf life: 6 weeks

150g/5½oz coconut oil
450g/1lb/generous 2 cups
   granulated sugar
Zest of 1 orange
Juice of 1 pomegranate

Make a double boiler by placing a glass bowl over a pan of simmering water. Allow the water to lap at the bowl, but not to flow over the edges of the pan. Add the coconut oil and allow to melt. Once the coconut oil has melted, remove the bowl from the pan (take care – it will be hot), allow to cool a little (but don't let it re-solidify) and then stir in the granulated sugar until all the grains are coated in the oil.

Add the orange zest and pomegranate juice, and stir through until fully combined. Allow to set, stirring occasionally as it does so, so that all the grains of sugar become coated in the oil and juice, fully incorporating everything until it firms up.

To use, scoop out a little of the scrub and rub it gently in your hands to loosen the coconut oil again, then apply to your skin.

*Add a few drops of vanilla essential oil to the mixture if you like, for added relaxing effects.

Coco Blast Body Scrub

In case it hasn't been obvious so far – I'm addicted to coconuts! I love everything about these babies, and when it comes to beauty, they're an all-rounder. This recipe is my favourite treat for myself (yes, I also like to make gifts on 'Celebrate Alex Day') and it smells amazing. Before a relaxing bath I'll rub this scrub all over my body, then sink into the warm water and pretend I'm on an island filled with coconuts.

Makes about 300ml/10½fl oz/
scant 1¼ cups
Shelf life: 3 months

50g/1¾oz coconut oil
50g/1¾oz/¼ cup coconut sugar
50g/1¾oz/¼ cup brown granulated
sugar
1 tbsp Himalayan pink salt crystals
or coarse sea salt (optional)
3 tbsp coconut cream
25g/1oz/¼ cup desiccated coconut
2 drops bergamot essential oil

Make a double boiler by placing a glass bowl over a pan of simmering water. Allow the water to lap at the bowl, but not to flow over the edges of the pan. Add the coconut oil and allow to melt. When the oil has completely melted, remove the bowl from the pan (take care – it will be hot) and allow the oil to cool slightly, but not so much that it resolidifies. Add the two sugars and stir to fully coat the sugar crystals in the oil. Add in the salt crystals, if using, the coconut cream, desiccated coconut and bergamot essential oil and stir again.

Store in an airtight jar in a warm room. To use, scoop out a little of the scrub and warm it gently in your hands to loosen the coconut oil again, then apply to your body.

Spiced Coffee Rejuvenating Body Oil

Homemade scented oils make a great gift for everyone, no matter what their age. You can personalize them by choosing essential oils and other ingredients to suit the giftee. This particular version makes a fab massage oil, too – it's soothing, calming and smells amazing!

Makes about 200ml/7fl oz/scant 1 cup
Shelf life: 4–6 months

125ml/4½fl oz/½ cup apricot kernel oil
125ml/4½fl oz/½ cup grapeseed oil
3 tbsp orange water (optional)
1 tbsp black filter coffee, cooled
3 tbsp pomegranate seeds
1 vanilla pod, split lengthways
8 cardamom pods, bruised
1 tsp whole cloves
1 tsp whole allspice berries
1 cinnamon stick

Make a double boiler by placing a glass bowl over a pan of simmering water. Allow the water to lap at the bowl, but not to flow over the edges of the pan. Add the apricot kernel and grapeseed oils, then add the orange water (if using), coffee, seeds and spices. With the heat very low, leave the flavours and goodness to infuse the oil – aim for 45–60 minutes on the heat. Check the bowl regularly, though, to make sure the oil isn't starting to bubble – be gentle and patient.

When the oil is smelling delicious, remove the bowl from the pan (take care – it will be hot) and leave the infusion to cool completely. Strain through a fine sieve or muslin into a clean glass bowl, then use a funnel to transfer the oil infusion to a cosmetics bottle, ideally one with a slow-flow cap. Store in a cool, dark place. To use, pour a small amount of the oil into the palm of your hand, rubbing your hands together briefly to warm the oil before massaging it into your skin.

This makes a wonderful gift – especially at Christmas. Instead of using plastic cosmetics bottles, pour the oil into clear, sterilized jars and add a few of the whole spices for decoration. Replace the lid and add a label.

Revitalizing Body Butter

The best thing about this recipe is its shelf life; this body butter will last up to 12 months, by which time you should have finished the whole jar and be ready to make a new batch.

Makes about 500ml/17fl oz/2 cups
Shelf life: 6–12 months

100g/3½oz coconut oil
100g/3½oz mango butter
100g/3½oz shea butter
100g/3½oz cocoa butter
80ml/2½fl oz/⅓ cup jojoba oil
1 tsp extra virgin olive oil
2 drops peppermint essential oil
2 drops rosemary essential oil

Make a double boiler by placing a glass bowl over a pan of simmering water. Allow the water to lap at the bowl, but not to flow over the edges of the pan. Add the coconut oil, and mango, shea and cocoa butters to the bowl and allow the ingredients to melt. Remove the bowl from the pan (take care – it will be hot) and allow to cool a little. Add the jojoba oil, olive oil and the essential oils, and stir to combine thoroughly. Allow the mixture to cool thoroughly in the bowl, then place the bowl in the fridge for about 45–60 minutes to chill until it becomes the consistency of dairy butter.

Remove the butter from the fridge and use a hand-held electric whisk to whip it until it is fluffy and light, like cotton-wool clouds of whipped cream. Transfer the body butter to a jar or other sealable container and store at room temperature.

*If you can't find mango butter, replace it with the same amount of shea or cocoa butter instead.

Gentle Vegan Body Butter

Makes about 300ml/10½fl oz/
    scant 1¼ cups
Shelf life: 4 months

125g/4½oz coconut oil
125ml/4fl oz/½ cup kukui nut oil
    or grapeseed oil
30g/1oz soy wax or candelilla wax
1 tsp vitamin E oil
4 drops geranium essential oil

I originally developed this body butter for babies, but I loved it so much that I now use it all the time on my own body. It is so soothing and nourishing – perfect for sensitive skin, and best of all it uses soy or candelilla wax, rather than beeswax, making it suitable for vegans, too. If you would like to use it as a baby lotion, geranium essential oil is mild and gentle and should be fine for babies over the age of six months. However, as with any baby product, always do a patch test first. Put a little on the baby's ankle and leave it for an hour: if there's any problem, a dab of witch hazel followed by some aloe vera gel will fix it right up.

Sterilize a large jar (see page 23) with a secure lid (a Kilner jar is perfect). Place the sterilized jar in a pan and fill the pan with water so that it comes up to the neck of the jar. Remove the jar and place the pan of water on the hob over a medium heat.

Place all the ingredients apart from the geranium essential oil in the jar and use a the handle of a wooden spoon to turn them through to roughly combine. Place the lid on the jar without securing it (leave it sitting on top of the neck of the jar, rather than screwing it on, for example) and place the jar in the saucepan of water. As the water heats up around the jar, the contents of the jar will start to melt – you can give them a stir with the long spoon handle every now and then to help things along, if you like.

Once the contents of the jar are completely melted, remove the jar from the water (use a tea towel as the jar will be hot), add the essential oil, put the lid on the jar and give it a shake to make sure everything is fully combined, then allow to cool. Store at room temperature and use as needed.

*Soy wax and candelilla wax are vegan alternatives to beeswax – for a non-vegan version substitute beeswax in equal measure.

Healing Body Butter

If you're prone to body break-outs then this one's for you: nourishing, antibacterial and healing, you can have smooth skin while secretly correcting those irritating blemishes. Best of all – you'll need to use it only twice a week.

Makes about 200ml/7fl oz/
   scant 1 cup
Shelf life: 6–12 months

90g/3oz cocoa butter
125g/4oz coconut oil
2 tbsp jojoba oil
20 drops tea tree oil

Melt the cocoa butter and coconut oil together in a small saucepan until dissolved. Add the jojoba oil, stir to combine, then leave in the pan overnight to cool completely and start to solidify. In the morning, place the pan in the fridge for 15–20 minutes to properly firm up.

Place the hardened mixture into a mixer and whip for 6–10 minutes like you would a cake batter (being sure to scrape down the sides). Add the tea tree oil and mix one last time, then transfer to an airtight container to store until needed.

Sunburnt Skin Rescue

There's nothing worse than a sunburn and I'm grateful to say I've been burnt badly only once in my life, but boy was that enough! Several days of being unable to lie on my front or back or on either side and I certainly learnt my lesson. This recipe is hydrating and restorative to help heal all those traumatized cells and replenish lost moisture.

Makes about 150ml/5fl oz/
scant ⅔ cup
Shelf life: 3 months

1½ tsp dried elderflowers
60ml/2fl oz/¼ cup aloe vera gel
1 tbsp witch hazel
2 tsp calendula oil
10 drops geranium essential oil

Place the elderflowers in a small cup and cover with 60ml/2fl oz/¼ cup boiling water. Allow the water to infuse for 10 minutes, then strain the liquid into a fresh cup and set aside to cool completely.

Once the elderflower infusion is cool, place the aloe vera gel, witch hazel, calendula oil and geranium essential oil in a glass bowl and stir to combine. Add the infusion and stir again.

Pour the mixture into a plastic cosmetics bottle with a spray top. Give it a shake to make sure everything is fully mixed together. To use, spray the soother liberally on the affected patches of skin. Store the spray in the fridge and shake again before each use.

*Elderflowers contain bioflavonoids that help to soothe the skin and reduce inflammation, which earns them their status as a remedy for sunburn.

The 'Anti' Antiperspirant

I've been using this deodorant for years in place of store-bought: most commercial deodorants contain aluminium, which I'm not so keen to have absorbed into my body. If you have an old stick deodorant container lying around you can pour this mixture straight in, leave it to set and use it in the usual way.

Makes 3–4 deodorant sticks
Shelf life: 6 months

125g/4oz coconut oil
125g/4oz beeswax or candelilla wax
150g/5oz mango butter
1 tbsp sweet almond oil
3 tbsp bicarbonate
   of soda (baking soda)
125g/4oz arrowroot powder
3 probiotics capsules, opened,
   powder reserved and capsules
   discarded
5 drops each of the following
   essential oils: lemon, grapefruit,
   lime, cypress, or 20 drops of your
   favourite essential oil

Make a double boiler by placing a glass bowl over a pan of simmering water. Allow the water to lap at the bowl, but not to flow over the edges of the pan. Add the coconut oil, beeswax and mango butter and allow them to melt. Once they have liquefied, stir to combine and remove the bowl from the pan (take care – it will be hot). Allow the mixture to cool, but not so that it re-solidifies (although cool enough that the heat doesn't destroy the beneficial properties of the probiotics).

Add the remaining ingredients, then gently stir to combine until you have a thick, pourable mixture. Pour it into empty stick deodorant containers (you can buy these online, or use cleaned-out used ones). Leave the deodorant at room temperature with the lids off the containers overnight to set. Use as you would a shop-bought stick deodorant.

#everyonelovesaquickie The quickest, easiest, no-fuss deodorant is lime juice. Just juice one whole lime, strain the pulp and seeds and transfer to a spray bottle. Apply as you would normal deodorant. (Best to wait 15 minutes after shaving as it will sting.)

LIPS & MOUTH

#totallykissable

When I walk down the toothpaste aisle at the supermarket I'm baffled by the crazy array of pastes, gels and mouth washes on offer (toothpaste with added glitter, anyone?). Looking after your mouth health is important, but all you really need is a simple toothpaste and mouth wash, both of which can be whipped up in a matter of minutes in the comfort of your kitchen.

There's also an obsession around whiter-than-white teeth these days and no end of products and procedures to get them that seem to cost a bomb. Before you splash out, check the contents of your fridge because you've probably already got the secret ingredient for an ace DIY whitener… revealed in a few pages!

Of course, keeping your lips soft and moisturized is important, too, so I've included a homemade lip scrub and lip balm to keep that pout looking prepped and polished.

X

Spearmint Lip Scrub

Our lips can get dry and dull, just like any other part of the body, so need exfoliating from time to time, too. Get to work with this lip scrub and you'll be a smooth operator again in no time.

Makes about 15ml/½fl oz/1 tbsp
Shelf life: 3 months

1 tsp coconut oil
½ tsp grapeseed oil
½ tsp honey, preferably raw
1 tsp golden granulated sugar
1 drop spearmint essential oil

Coconut oil is pretty solid, but you don't need to melt it in this recipe. Put both oils and the honey in a small glass bowl and work them together with the back of a spoon to fully combine. Add the sugar and work again, making sure all the grains of sugar are coated in the oil and honey mixture. Finally add the essential oil and work again. Transfer to a lip-balm jar and store in a warm room.

*You can use jojoba or sweet almond oil instead of coconut oil, if you prefer. In this case, though, double the quantity of honey to 1 tsp.

Tropical Lip Balm

I always carry a small jar of lip balm in my handbag to keep my lips moist, particularly during winter. Lips serve important functions, from eating to kissing, and they need a good condition every now and then!

Makes about 40g/1½oz
Shelf life: 6 months

2 tsp coconut oil
2 tsp apricot kernel oil
15g/½oz beeswax
2 tsp mango butter
½ tsp aloe vera gel
½ tsp vitamin E oil
5 drops tangerine essential oil
4 drops passionfruit essential oil
(optional)

Make a double boiler by placing a glass bowl over a pan of simmering water. Allow the water to lap at the bowl, but not to flow over the edges of the pan. Add the apricot kernel oil, coconut oil, beeswax, and mango butter and allow to melt. Remove the bowl from the pan (take care – the bowl will be hot) and add the aloe vera, vitamin E oil, tangerine essential oil and passionfruit essential oil (if using). Stir to combine, then transfer to a lip-balm jar (you may need more than one, depending upon the size) and leave for about 10–20 minutes to set. Store at room temperature.

#everyonelovesaquickie A little coconut oil or shea butter works as an all-purpose lip balm if that's all you have to hand.

Peppermint Toothpaste

Makes about 60ml/2fl oz/¼ cup
Shelf life: 24 months

1½ tbsp powdered bentonite clay
    (see safety note, page 26)
2 tbsp filtered water
1 tbsp coconut oil
2 tsp bicarbonate of soda
    (baking soda)
5 drops peppermint essential oil

This toothpaste removes bacteria, plaque and germs and the bicarb keeps teeth white and stain free.

Mix the clay and water in a plastic bowl with a wooden or plastic spoon to form a paste. Add the remaining ingredients and mix well to fully combine.

Clay toothpaste can take a little getting used to as it feels a bit like brushing your teeth with dirt, so please persevere. If you need to make it more palatable, just add extra peppermint. It's also important not to scrub your teeth: a gentle brush is fine.

#everyonelovesaquickie Running behind? Use bicarbonate of soda and water or straight coconut oil to keep your teeth clean.

*Bentonite clay can react with metal and cause toxicity (see page 26). If you have any metal fillings replace the bentonite in this recipe with the same quantity of Redmond clay or activated charcoal.

Minty Antibacterial Mouth Wash

Store-bought mouth wash is loaded with nasties but you can make your own all-natural version in less than a minute.

Makes about 375ml/13fl oz/1½ cups
Shelf life: 6 months

375ml/13fl oz/1½ cups green tea, cooled
1 tsp bicarbonate of soda (baking soda)
1 tsp calcium, magnesium & zinc powder
3 drops peppermint essential oil
2 drops tea tree essential oil
2 drops rosemary essential oil

Pour the green tea into a glass bowl, add the bicarbonate of soda and calcium, magnesium & zinc powder and stir to combine, making sure you get rid of any lumps. Add the essential oils and stir again. Transfer the mouth wash to a glass or plastic bottle and give it a shake to make sure it's fully combined.

To use, shake again, then take a mouthful and swish it around your teeth and gums, making sure to push the mouth wash through your teeth. Spit, then rinse your mouth with fresh water.

*Calcium, magnesium & zinc powder is easily available online or at your local pharmacy. In a mouth wash it helps to protect the enamel on your teeth.

WHITEN TEETH WITH STRAWBERRIES

We've gone a bit overboard for teeth whitening treatments in recent years, but there's no need to splurge on expensive, harsh procedures when a simple (and delicious!) DIY alternative might already be sitting in your fridge. I'm talking about strawberries – yes, strawberries! These little beauties contain malic, an astringent which can remove surface discolouration on teeth. Take a couple of strawberries and mash them to a fine pulp. Add ½ tbsp of baking soda and blend well. Spread this mixture over your teeth with a soft toothbrush or clean finger. Leave for 5 minutes before rinsing your mouth out thoroughly with milk or water.

NOTE: this treatment is so effective that you shouldn't use it more than once a week or you might damage your tooth enamel.

CELLULITE BE GONE

#thedirtiestofdirtywords

It doesn't matter what size or shape they are, all my female friends complain of the dreaded cellulite. It really is something that plagues all of us women so please don't be fooled by the airbrushed thighs of the models you see in magazines (trust me, they're not perfect either).

In simple terms, cellulite is caused by fat deposits under the skin that push the surrounding connective tissue out of shape. It tends to hit the hips, thighs and butt the worst. Diet and lifestyle can contribute to cellulite but so can hormones and genetics, so there's little point beating yourself up about it.

Having said that, there are things we can do to improve the appearance of dimply skin, and they don't have to come with a hefty price tag.

Running, swimming and brisk walking are all good forms of exercise for cellulite – they get the blood pumping to those stubborn areas of your body and help to loosen the fat deposits there. Sitting still for long periods won't help so if you work a desk job, take lots of regular breaks – walk over to your colleague and talk to them instead of sending an email!

You can also give the following natural remedies a whirl – there are a bunch of quick fixes, or why not try rubbing coffee over your butt instead of drinking it – it will probably do you more good!

X

Just for the Ladies

There are so many wonderful things about being a woman and a ton
of experiences we get to have that men will never really understand, but we also
find ourselves subjected to a heck of a lot of pressures.

Magazines, models, film stars and the like all appear to be perfect: they enter
and exit pregnancy unflawed, without a glimmer of a stretch mark, they parade
down the beach in the teensiest of bikinis with washboard abs and dimple-free thighs
and they never, ever have fuzz that grows in places it shouldn't. Talk about
an unobtainable ideal.

Here's the scoop – all those flawless ladies gracing the red carpet and the cover of
Vogue are subjecting themselves to beauty torture each and every day: waxing,
shaving, plucking, laser and bleach; lipo sculpting, Venus freeze and endermologie;
wraps and scrubs and special massages; detox after detox, personal training
sessions, sweating it up in the sauna; layers and layers of make-up designed to
streamline any flaws... and that's before all those pretty pictures are retouched
and colour corrected.

I promise it's not a life to envy, but we are women and we like to look and feel our best (and why shouldn't we? We work our butts off – literally!)

This section is for all the women, young or old, who want a few tips and tricks for feeling confident in their own skin. I too know what it's like to be dissatisfied with my appearance and I spend hours every day hearing critique after critique on everything from my height to my freckles. I have hair that grows in places I think it shouldn't, I have stretch marks from growth spurts and pregnancy and I've suffered the bane of cellulite in my life.

I've been testing these recipes for years and I hope they will give you the confidence to feel beautiful in your own skin.

X

Cellulite Busters

#everyonelovesaquickie

Use a Body Brush

Dry brushing is a really cheap and effective way to tackle cellulite. Get yourself a body brush with soft bristles and be sure to use it dry (the clue's in the name). You can body brush daily and the best time to do it is before you step into your morning shower.

Brush in long sweeps towards the heart to stimulate your circulation and lymphatic system, releasing toxins and aiding digestion. You'll also clean the pores and treat your to a skin a gentle exfoliation. Starting at your feet, brush up each leg and over the thighs and buttocks, then work from wrists to shoulders. Move the brush anti-clockwise on your stomach and avoid the delicate skin in the breast area. Don't brush too hard – we want to stimulate the skin, not irritate it.

Scrub with Coffee

Save up your coffee grounds and use them to make this simple home remedy. The caffeine in the coffee helps to stimulate the circulation and tighten the skin; the exfoliating action regenerates skin cells.

Combine ¼ cup coffee grounds with 3 tbsp brown sugar and 2 tbsp melted coconut oil to create a paste. Massage into the affected areas of the skin for a few minutes before washing off. Repeat 3 times per week.

Eat Omega-3s

Cellulite is the result of fat cells putting strain on connective tissue in your skin. Eating a diet rich in healthy omega-3 fatty acids (found in oily fish, nuts and seeds) helps make your skin stronger and more elastic. Which is altogether bad news for skin-dimpling.

Drink Green Tea

While we're talking about coffee, it's best not to drink too much of it because a high caffeine intake can contribute to cellulite (seems it's more beneficial ON the body than INSIDE it – go figure). Stick to one cup of coffee a day maximum and then opt for green tea instead – it contains powerful antioxidants called catechins that help to remove toxins from the body.

Take Gelatin

Gelatin is a great source of dietary collagen, the protein that the body needs to build cells, tissues and organs. It supports skin, hair and nail growth and can help to tighten the skin and reduce the appearance of cellulite.

Years ago our diets would have included way more gelatin from eating all the parts of the animal, but these days the most delicious way to consume it is probably from eating a nourishing bone broth. Unless you're into that (and even if you are, I doubt you'd want to eat it every day), you can take gelatin capsules, available from the health-food store, as a supplement.

Detox in the Bath

Epsom salts work wonders for reducing puffiness and drawing toxins from the body. Bathing in them is a super-relaxing way to fight cellulite. Simply add ½ cup to your bath and soak away for 20 minutes.

After bathing (or showering), make sure you moisturize – always! If you don't have time to make up one of the luxurious body butters in this book, a dollop of coconut oil will work wonders.

Coconut Coffee Scrub Cakes for Cellulite

Sometimes I think my freezer works just as hard as I do! I mean who knew you could blitz cellulite, stretch marks and even puffy faces with a coconut-oil frozen cupcake? I'm a big fan of the big C oil, also known as the eighth wonder of the world – it's perfect for repairing skin tears (a.k.a. stretch marks) and providing essential moisture. I love how silky my skin feels when I'm done with these scrub cakes.

Makes about 6 cakes
Shelf life: 8 weeks (in the freezer)

150g/5½oz coconut oil
275g/9¾oz fresh coffee grounds

Make a double boiler by placing a glass bowl over a pan of simmering water. Allow the water to lap at the bowl, but not to flow over the edges of the pan. Place 125g/4½oz coconut oil in the bowl and allow it to melt. Once it has liquefied, add 125g/4½oz of the coffee grounds and stir well to combine.

Remove the bowl from the pan (take care – it will be hot) and divide the mixture in equal amounts into holes of a muffin tin (the oil will rise and form a creamy layer on the surface as the mixture cools). Replace the bowl back on the pan and add the remaining coconut oil, allowing it to melt. Stir in the remaining coffee grounds and remove the bowl from the pan again. Divide the thicker coffee mixture equally between each muffin hole, spreading it over each cake and pressing it down firmly with the back of a spoon. Allow the cakes to set at room temperature (or in the fridge if it's warm out).

Once the cakes are set, pop them out of the tin and into a resealable bag, then store them in the freezer. To use, take one cake into the shower and use it as a body scrub. Don't forget to rinse your skin thoroughly afterwards, and to follow up with moisturizer.

SO LONG
STRETCH MARKS
#astretchintimesavesnine

'I'm so in awe of the incredible miracle my body went through; all I cared about was the health of my child and this amazing experience. I totally didn't care if I got stretch marks.'

I hate this line! Usually used by celebrity (and model) mums who were completely unphased by pregnancy and stretch marks yet magically didn't end up with a blemish – what a load of rubbish. What they didn't tell you about were the hours of rubbing various butters and creams into their growing bellies to ensure the skin stayed moist and less prone to tearing, or the sneaky little laser procedures post baby to remove any unsightly purple marks.

I've had stretch marks for as long as I can remember; they're not caused by just pregnancy or extreme weight gain, they're also caused by growing. I hit my current height aged 10 (making me freakishly tall for a young person) and I remember all too well the hours of agony as my limbs and skin stretched and grew. It was painful enough without being left with all those tiny reminders taking residency on my hips. These days, however, I have hardly any tears visible on my skin thanks to some home remedies courtesy of my Nan, and a few other natural fixes I've stumbled upon over the years.

Whether your battle wounds are fresh and purple or faded and silvery, any and all of these quickie recipes can yield great results (obviously the older the marks are, the more love they're going to need, so please persevere for at least six weeks to see maximum benefits).

X

Stretch Mark Savers
#everyonelovesaquickie

Olive Oil
Rich in antioxidants and nutrients, olive oil aids the regeneration of cells, which helps restore the skin to its pre-tear glory. Warm a few tablespoons of oil, then massage it gently into the affected area until completely absorbed.

Alfalfa Leaves
These contain amino acids and vitamins E and K, which improve skin health and tone. Mix 1 tsp alfalfa powder (available online and at health-food stores) with a few drops of argan oil to form a paste. Gently massage into the affected area twice a day.

Sugar
A natural exfoliant for skin, sugar is one of the best home remedies to get rid of stretch marks. Take 1 tbsp of granulated sugar and add a few drops of almond oil and lemon juice. Rub into the affected area for 10 minutes and then rinse.

Aloe Vera

One of the most effective home remedies for stretch marks and skin problems. Apply aloe vera gel to the affected area and massage gently until completely absorbed.

Lemon Juice

The acid in lemon juice helps fade stretch marks and scars. Squeeze the juice from one lemon and massage into the affected area for 10 minutes, then rinse with warm water.

Cocoa Butter

This has such a great reputation for enhancing blood circulation, which helps to reduce the appearance of stretch marks and prevent them from appearing (great for use during pregnancy). Massage a small amount of cocoa butter into the affected area twice a day for two months.

Egg Whites

Rich in proteins, egg whites can help to restore skin's elasticity and increase the production of collagen. Whisk the whites of 2 eggs and massage into the affected area for 10 minutes, then rinse.

Potato Juice

The juice from potatoes is rich in minerals and vitamins. It promotes restoration and growth of skin cells. Cut a few thick slices of a medium-sized potato and gently rub the slices into the affected area until they become dry, then rinse and apply a light layer of moisturizer.

STAYING
FUZZ-FREE
#hairremovalhacks

You know that moment when your best friend confesses to a
'slightly embarrassing' beauty secret and you shrink back and think to yourself,
'Oh my gosh! I can't believe she just admitted that!' and then immediately,
'Why didn't I know about this?!'

Call us crazy, but we're confessing. Every inside tip, tried-and-trusted technique,
helpful tool and newfangled beauty solution. WHY? So you learn something new.
For all the girlfriends who are wondering and our friends who won't ask.
So you can look and feel your best.

X

To Bleach Or Not To Bleach?

Let's start with the real deal. If we were all sisters, we'd have to be honest and say it: 'tache bleaching doesn't work. In fact, it highlights the tiny hairs you are trying to hide. Not to mention that slathering a harsh chemical agent on your skin is not exactly a healthy choice. So, friends, let's put down the bleach once and for all. Here's a breakdown of three solutions to staying fuzz-free.

SUGARING

What is it? A technique of waxing using a sugar, honey and lemon solution formed into a sugar paste.

What to expect The wax paste is applied to the desired area and removed in one fell swoop. Also great for eyebrows and the bikini area.

Why the hype? This sugary solution sticks to the hair without bonding to your skin, therefore creating less chance for irritation. Because the wax is applied by hand and not a stick and then covered by a cloth strip, the aesthetician can be more precise and create cleaner lines.

Chic tip If you like to wax, give this natural option a try.

THREADING

What is it? A thin cotton string is doubled and twisted and then rolled over hair, plucking it from the root in a straight line.

What to expect? Typically the threader has one end of the string in each hand and the middle portion in her mouth. You'll sit back in the chair and hold your skin taut. Pain is minimal and the entire process takes less than 10 minutes. Also great for eyebrows.

Why the hype? This ancient eastern tradition is legit. And it's making waves across the wild, wild west. It removes hair in a clean, straight line and even manages to grab the tiniest hairs. With no product adhering to the skin, threading offers little to no irritation and minimal redness.

Chic tip This method is the most cost-effective in my book and the results last for up to three weeks.

LASER TREATMENT

What is it? A concentrated beam of light targets hair and damages the follicle, stunting future growth.

What to expect The desired area is treated multiple times depending on how coarse and dense the hair. The bark is worse than the bite though. The fancy lasers look scary, but it feels only like a small slap from a rubber band when it hits the skin.

Why the hype? The newfangled treatment gets better and better over time and for many people it really works.

The downside? Price and unpredictability.

Alex weighs in On a consultation I was given the price range of about £1,250/$1,600 US/$2,100 AUS for five treatments without a guarantee that the hair would not grow back.

My Favourite Homemade Shaving Cream

I'm a shaving cream gal from way back and I personally think nothing provides a more thorough shave than using a cream. I first came up with this recipe because I was often shaving my legs in a hurry and didn't have time to apply a moisturizer, which left my fuzz-free limbs feeling dry and flaky. This recipe has cocoa butter to nourish the skin and keep you hair-free for longer. I've tested this on all the women (and men) I know and they all agree it's the best shave they've ever had.

Makes about 200ml/7fl oz/
   scant 1 cup
Shelf life: 9 months

2 tbsp cocoa butter
4 tbsp jojoba or sweet almond oil
4 tbsp liquid Castile soap
1 tsp raw honey
1 tsp bicarbonate
   of soda (baking soda)
20 drops orange essential oil

Make a double boiler by placing a glass bowl over a pan of simmering water. Allow the water to lap at the bowl, but not to flow over the edges of the pan. Add the cocoa butter and jojoba or sweet almond oil, allow to melt, then remove the bowl (take care – the bowl will be hot) and set aside to cool.

In separate bowl, put 200ml/7fl oz/¾ cup + 2 tbsp filtered water and add the Castile soap and raw honey. Add the bicarbonate of soda and stir until dissolved.

Pour the butter and oil mixture into the soap mixture, add the essential oils and pour the lot into a blender (a little at a time or you'll end up with this all over the worktop). Blend for 20 seconds until foamy. Pour into your container of choice and continue until all the mixture has been blended.

---

*Traditional shaving cream contains a whole host of nasties, but the one that bothers me most is butane, a.k.a. lighter fluid. It's what gives it that foaming pump but it's ridiculously dangerous and should be avoided at all costs.

#everyonelovesaquickie You can shave with straight coconut oil if you don't have shaving cream handy. It will completely transform your skin and leave it glowing and silky smooth.

#hisandherhacks SHAVE PROPERLY

Beards are big news these days, with everyone from movie stars to hipsters sporting them. But there are times when only a baby-smooth face will do so here are my top tips for a good shave – ladies, you can also learn from these as they apply to shaving other body parts, too!

TAKE YOUR TIME
Rushing a shave is one of the biggest causes of nicks, so set aside enough time to do it properly.

SHAVE IN THE SHOWER...
Ever tried shaving in the shower? The hot water and steam will open up your pores and give your skin and hair a chance to soften, reducing the chances of ingrown hair and nicks.

... OR USE THE HOT CLOTH METHOD
If you don't have time to shower, boil a kettle and fill a large bowl with boiling water. Put a clean washcloth in the water and leave the water to cool a little. Then wring out the washcloth and lay it over your face for a few minutes until it cools.

PREPARATION, PREPARATION
Whether you're shaving in the shower or not, wash your face to get rid of any dirt and crumbs from your stubble. Even better – use a gentle exfoliator to prevent ingrown hairs and give you a clean canvas to work with.

FORGET THE FOAM
Cheap shaving foams can dry out and irritate the skin so stick to an all-natural shaving cream – or make your own (see opposite and on page 118).

USE A SHARP BLADE
Invest in a good quality razor and look after it – a new, sharp, clean blade is essential for a smooth shave. Work with the grain, not against it and don't put too much pressure on the blade – glide, don't scrape!

AFTERCARE
Rinse your face and neck with plenty of cool water and apply a gentle, all-natural post-shave moisturizing lotion.

Easy DIY Shaving Cream

If you need a no-brainer then this one's for you; it's actually the shaving cream I started with. One of my best friends has had a shaved head since as long as I can remember and this is the recipe he uses to keep his scalp nourished. Man or woman, head or legs, if you've got skin on the drier side, then you can't go wrong with this.

Makes about 375ml/13fl oz/
   1½ cups
Shelf life: 9 months

250g/9oz shea butter
125g/4oz coconut oil
½ tsp sweet almond oil
7 drops rosemary essential oil
3 drops lavender essential oil
5 drops peppermint essential oil

Make a double boiler by placing a glass bowl over a pan of simmering water. Allow the water to lap at the bowl, but not to flow over the edges of the pan. Add the shea butter, coconut oil and jojoba oil and allow to melt. Once the butter and oil mixture is melted, give it a stir, remove the bowl from the heat (take care – it will be hot) and add the essential oils. Stir well to combine.

Leave the mixture to cool, then place in the fridge for 10–15 minutes until it has firmed up a bit. Once the mixture is firm, remove the bowl from the fridge and beat the mixture with a hand-held electric whisk, until it is soft set, like the consistency of softened (dairy) butter. Transfer the shaving cream to an airtight container and store at room temperature.

Bikini Beautiful Skin Mask

It's probably no secret that my job prefers a clean (shaven) canvas, plus in this era it seems everyone is shaving, waxing or IPL'ing something or other. Why go to all that effort just to end up with lumps and bumps where pesky little hairs fight for daylight? We mask our faces, right? Why not our lady zone? This mask speeds up healing, calms any post-wax redness, reduces swelling, kills infection, and works in 20 minutes.

Makes about 150ml/5fl oz/
scant ⅔ cup
Shelf life: 2 weeks

50g/2oz/½ cup kaolin clay
2 tsp bee pollen
2 tsp kelp powder
¼ tsp vitamin C powder
1 tsp raw honey
1 tsp sunflower oil
5 drops extra-virgin olive oil
4 drops bee propolis
2 drops myrtle essential oil
2 drops ravensara essential oil
2 drops tea tree essential oil
3 drops ylang ylang essential oil

Boil a kettle of fresh water. Allow the water to cool until it is just warm.

Put the clay, pollen, and kelp and vitamin C powders in a glass bowl and stir to combine. Add the honey, and sunflower and olive oils and stir again, then add the bee propolis and the essential oils. Stir everything thoroughly so that you have a homogeneous mixture. Once everything is mixed together well, add the warm water, a little at a time and stirring between each addition, until you've created a thick but spreadable paste. Don't be put off by the distinctive smell – that's the bee propolis: you just have to trust it's doing you good.

To use, spread the paste evenly with your fingers over your bikini line (and any other shaved bits!). Leave the mask in place for 15–20 minutes, then rinse off with warm water and moisturize.

---

*Bee propolis is a type of glue made from flower and tree sap. It has incredible benefits for your skin including the regeneration of cells and tissue as well as purifying and helping draw out the gunk inside clogged pores (a.k.a. ingrowns). You can buy it online and at some health-food stores.

#everyonelovesaquickie Short on time? Just make a clay and water paste: 1 tsp kaolin clay to 1 tbsp warm water and apply to the affected area. Let dry, then rinse and moisturize.

Directory

Organic Supermarkets & Online Suppliers

Amazon (worldwide) www.amazon.com
Health Emporium, The (AU) www.healthemporium.com.au
Mr Vitamins (AU) www.mrvitamins.com.au
Planet Organic (UK) www.planetorganic.com
Westerly Natural Market (USA) www.westerlynaturalmarket.com
Wholefoods Market (UK/USA/Canada) www.wholefoodsmarket.com

Cosmetic Ingredient Suppliers

From Nature with Love (USA) www.fromnaturewithlove.com
Holland & Barrett (UK) www.hollandandbarrett.com
Mountain Rose Herbs (USA) www.mountainroseherbs.com
New Directions (AU) www.newdirections.com.au
New Directions Aromatics (UK) www.newdirectionsuk.com
Nikita Naturals (AU) www.nikitanaturals.com
Skin Essential Actives (ASIA) www.skinessentialactives.com

Bottles & Packaging Suppliers

All In Packaging (UK) www.allinpackaging.co.uk
Escentials of Australia (AU) www.escentialsofaustralia.com
Just Jars (AU) www.justjars.com.au
SKS Bottles (USA) www.sks-bottle.com
World of Bottles (UK) www.world-of-bottles.co.uk

Worldwide Natural Beauty Suppliers

The Model Handmade www.themodelhandmade.com
100% Pure www.100percentpure.com
Lush www.lush.com.au
Morrocco Method www.morroccomethod.com

Acknowledgements

A huge thank you to my incredible family and friends, without whom this book would never have been written.

To my mum, for your never ending wisdom and for making so many of these recipes with me (even though you hate cooking).

My soul mate, life guru and sister, Stephanie, for testing each and every one of my creations so diligently and for encouraging me to put my scribbled bits of paper into a book.

To my little Yorkie, Rosie, who reminds me every day that animals are to be loved and never test-subjects.

To Harley, thank you for teaching me what it means to be happy. All of this is all I have and all I have is yours.

To all the men and women who love and are learning to love themselves; may you be inspired and guided to nurture the most valuable asset you have – YOU!

And to my son, for inspiring and guiding me on this path; I am eternally grateful. We had a lifetime together in the space of a single moment and I will love you all the days of my life.

Index

a

acne 19
activated charcoal 96
after-shave balm 19
age spots 36
alcohol 6, 12, 13, 14, 23, 24, 32, 65
alfalfa leaves 110
allantoin 26
aloe vera 26, 32, 45, 60, 66, 74, 87, 88, 95, 111
amino acids 26, 27, 52, 110
antibacterial 18, 27, 78, 88, 98
antioxidants 11, 26, 27, 105, 110
antiperspirant 10, 69, 90
apple cider vinegar 14, 26, 34, 52
apricot kernal oil 60, 78, 84, 95
argan oil 60, 110
arrowroot powder 18, 26, 44, 48, 57, 90
avocado 60
avocado oil 12, 36

b

baby body butter 87
banana 13, 60
bath milk 70
bath salts 15, 23, 72, 105
beard care 117
bee pollen 26, 120
bee propolis 120
beeswax 12, 19, 27, 33, 37, 57, 74, 87, 90, 95
beetroot powder 12
BHA and BHT 10, 13
bicarbonate of soda 15, 26, 33, 48, 70, 72, 76, 90, 96, 98, 116
bikini lines 114, 120
bleach, hair 114
body butters 22, 86–8
body care 68–91
body conditioner 74
body oil 84
body scrubs 79, 81, 83, 105, 106
body wash 78
bubble bath 73

c

cancer 10, 11
carcinogens 10, 11, 12
Castile soap 14, 15, 19, 33, 34, 42, 44, 73, 78, 116
carrot seed oil 33
cedarwood oil 48
cellulite 6, 9, 100–107
cetearyl alcohol 11, 12, 13
chamomile 36, 53, 56, 76
chemicals 9–15, 26, 29, 32, 37, 41, 66
chlorine 21
cinnamon 47, 48, 84
clay 14, 15, 21, 26, 33, 47, 96, 120, 128
cocoa butter 12, 18, 19, 26, 86, 88, 111, 116
cocoa powder 48
coconut milk 42, 47
coconut oil 12, 14, 15, 18, 19, 36, 56, 60, 66, 70, 74, 81, 83, 86, 87, 88, 90, 94, 95, 96, 105, 106, 116, 118
coffee 20, 60, 84, 101, 105, 106
colour/colourants 10, 12, 26, 27, 45, 48, 60
containers 22–3
cucumber 13

d

dandruff 51, 57, 66
DEA ingredients 10, 14
deodorant 11, 18, 90
detox 15, 105
dibutyl phthalate (DBP) 9, 10
dry brushing 105

e

egg(s) 60, 11
emollients 11, 12, 52
emulsifiers 11, 13, 26, 36, 37, 74
Epsom salts 15, 27, 63, 70, 72, 105
equipment 20–21
essential fatty acids 26, 57
essential oils 13, 14, 18, 22, 27, 128
eye irritants 10, 11, 14

f

foot care 19, 79
formaldehyde 10, 15
fragrance 10, 13, 14, 18, 27

g

gelatin(e) 64, 105
ginger 37, 47
grapeseed oil 27, 32, 57, 84, 87, 94
green tea 98, 105

h

hair, ingrown 117, 120
hair care 38–67
hair colourants 45, 48, 60
hair conditioner 9, 14, 40, 41, 49, 54–7
hair gel 64
hair masks 58–61
hair removal 112–121
hair rinses 50–53
hair loss 6, 39, 41, 44, 51, 64
hair spray 65, 66
hair styling 62–7
hand care 28–37
hand lotion 36, 37
honey 14, 26, 27, 36, 37, 53, 60, 73, 78, 94, 114, 116, 120
hormones 101
humectants 12–13, 19

i

iron oxides 12

j

jojoba oil 12, 13, 19, 27, 44, 56, 63, 65, 79, 86, 88, 94, 116, 118

k

keratin 27

l

laser hair removal 115
lavender 36, 53, 56, 70, 73, 74, 76, 118
lemon 34, 53, 60, 64, 90, 110, 111, 114
limonene 11
linalool 11
lip balms 10, 19, 95
lip care 92–95
lip scrub 94
lipstick 10, 12
lye 30

m

magnesium 14, 27, 98,
mango butter 86, 90, 95
marshmallow root 57
masks 58–61, 120–21
mica powders 12
mint 32, 44, 79, 86, 94, 96, 98, 118
moisturizers
    body 74, 84–9
    hand 36–7
mouth wash 98

n

neroli essential oil 36, 74, 78

o

oils 12–14, 18, 19, 23, 27, 30, 40, 44, 66, 76,
    84, 128
omega-3 fatty acids 57
omega-6 fats 33
orange 57, 66, 72, 81,
organic products 11–14

p

parabens 10, 13
PEG compounds 10, 13, 14
peptides 27, 33, 37, 52
petrolatum 10, 12
phytokeratin 44, 52, 57
pomegranate 81, 84
pores 81, 105, 117, 120
potato juice 111
preservatives 10, 13
propylene glycol 11, 13, 14
pumpkin 60

r

relaxation 70, 73, 76, 81, 105
rice bran 13
rose 32, 74
rosehip 44
rosemary 44, 57, 65, 86, 98, 118

s

salt 15, 27, 63, 65, 66, 70, 72, 79, 83, 105
sandalwood 56–7
sanitizer, hand 32
saponin 27

scrubs 79–83, 94, 105, 106
sebum 27, 36
shampoo 9, 14, 19, 24, 38–49, 66
shaving 113–121
shea butter 12, 19, 27, 30, 33, 36, 74,
    86, 95, 118
silk 33, 37, 52
siloxanes 10
skin ageing 27, 33, 36, 37
soap 15, 19, 24, 27, 29, 30, 33, 34
sodium laureth/lauryl sulfate 10, 13, 14
solvents 10, 14
sterilization 23, 84, 87
strawberry 60, 99
stress relief 6, 11, 27, 79
stretch marks 9, 102–3, 108–11
sugar 15, 26, 27, 65, 66, 81, 83, 94, 105, 110
sugaring 114
sulphates 10, 14, 27, 44, 52
sunblock 27
sunburn 91, 166
surfactants 10, 14, 29
sweet almond oil 19, 37, 42, 48, 56, 60,
    73, 90, 94, 116, 118

t

tamanu oil 12
tea 53, 74, 98, 105
tea tree oil 14, 32, 44, 52, 79, 88, 98, 120
teeth whitening 99
thickeners 11, 14, 19, 27
threading 115
tocopheryl acetate 11
toner, hair 51
toothpaste, peppermint 96
triclosan 10

v

vanilla 13, 37, 45, 78, 81, 84
vegetable glycerine 13, 27, 30, 36, 37, 57
vitamin C powder 120
vitamin E 11, 32, 42, 44, 87, 95, 110

w

water intake 13, 14, 15, 21–3
water retention 72
waxes 12, 13, 19, 26, 27, 87
waxing 114, 120
witch hazel 87, 89

y

ylang ylang 8, 76, 78, 120
yogurt 60
yucca extract 14

z

zinc oxide 27, 48

#everyoneloves aquickie

Here's a handy reference guide for all you quickie fans!

Antiperspirant 90
Bath salts 72
Cellulite busters 104
Dry shampoo 48
Foaming dispenser 24
Hair conditioner 56
Hair masks 60
Hair rinse 52, 53
Hair styling 63
Hand lotion 36
Hand sanitizer 32
Hand soap 33
Hand wash 34
Lip balm 95
Mask for your bikini line 120
Shampoo 42
Shaving cream 116
Stretch mark savers 110–111
Toothpaste 96

PUBLISHER'S NOTES

Bentonite clay is used in several recipes in this book. Bentonite is a positively charged element which means it attaches to negative elements. It cannot come into contact with anything metallic or it becomes toxic. Recipes using bentonite must be made with wooden or plastic utensils.

Essential oils can be potent. Always read the labels before using, check for contraindications and ensure safe dilutions in a base oil or soap.

Neither the author nor the publisher can take any responsibility for any illness or injury caused as a result of following any of the advice or using any of the recipes or methods contained in this book.

PUBLISHER'S ACKNOWLEDGEMENTS

With thanks to photographer Rachel Whiting, and to stylist and home economist Aya Nishimura.

First published in the United Kingdom in 2017 by
Pavilion
43 Great Ormond Street
London
WC1N 3HZ

ISBN 978-1-91121-688-9

A CIP catalogue record for this book is available from the British Library.

10 9 8 7 6 5 4 3 2

The information and material provided in this publication is representative of the author's opinions and views. The information and material is presented in good faith; however, no warranty is given, nor are results guaranteed. Pavilion does not have any control over, or any responsibility for, any author or third party websites referred to in this book.

Reproduction by Mission Productions Ltd, Hong Kong
Printed and bound by 1010 Printing International Ltd, China

This book can be ordered direct from the publisher at www.pavilionbooks.com